basic Bitchen

basic bitchen

100+ EVERYDAY RECIPES *from*
NACHO AVERAGE NACHOS *to*
GOSSIP-WORTHY SUNDAY PANCAKES
for the BASIC BITCH IN YOUR LIFE

Joey Skladany

TILLER PRESS

NEW YORK   LONDON   TORONTO   SYDNEY   NEW DELHI

An Imprint of Simon & Schuster, Inc.
1230 Avenue of the Americas
New York, NY 10020

First Tiller Press hardcover edition May 2020

TILLER PRESS and colophon are trademarks of Simon & Schuster, Inc.

For information about special discounts for bulk purchases, please contact Simon & Schuster Special Sales at 1-866-506-1949 or business@simonandschuster.com.

The Simon & Schuster Speakers Bureau can bring authors to your live event. For more information or to book an event contact the Simon & Schuster Speakers Bureau at 1-866-248-3049 or visit our website at www.simonspeakers.com.

Cover design by Patrick Sullivan
Interior design by Matt Ryan
Recipes developed by Alexandra Utter
Photography by Davide Luciano
Food styling by Claudia Ficca
Prop styling by Maeve Sheridan

Manufactured in the United States of America.

10   9   8   7   6   5   4   3   2   1

Library of Congress Cataloging-in-Publication Data

Names: Skladany, Joey, author.
Title: Basic bitchen : 100+ everyday recipes-from nacho average nachos to gossip-worthy sunday pancakes-for the basic bitch in your life / Joey Skladany.
Description: New York : Tiller Press, 2020. | Includes index. | Summary: "100+ everyday recipes for every basic bitch in your life, complete with tips and tricks, by food writer, TV/radio personality and executive editor at Chowhound"--Provided by publisher.
Identifiers: LCCN 2019056188 (print) | LCCN 2019056189 (ebook) | ISBN 9781982138387 (hardback) | ISBN 9781982138400 (ebook)
Subjects: LCSH: Quick and easy cooking.
Classification: LCC TX833.5 .S583 2020 (print) | LCC TX833.5 (ebook) | DDC 641.5/12—dc23
LC record available at https://lccn.loc.gov/2019056188
LC ebook record available at https://lccn.loc.gov/2019056189

ISBN 978-1-9821-3838-7
ISBN 978-1-9821-3840-0 (ebook)

Contents

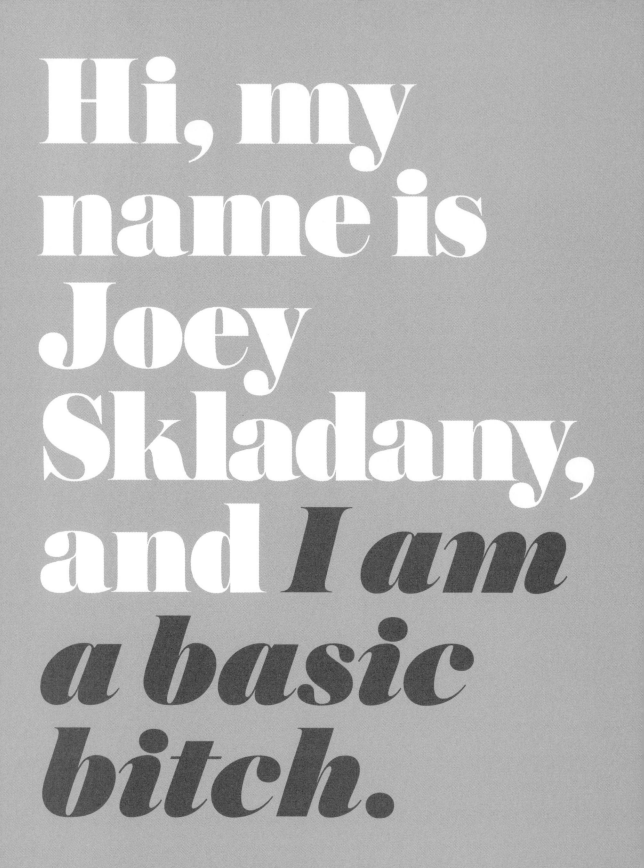

Hi, my name is Joey Skladany, and *I am a basic bitch.*

It didn't take Tory Burch flats and a twelve-step meeting to arrive at this conclusion, but the process of 1) acknowledgment and 2) wholehearted acceptance wasn't easy, given the term's negative association with vapid sorority girls void of any cultural exposure or influence. But in a society where everyone seeks to be special and prides themselves on their differences, there is one common bond that inevitably unites us all: basicness. And while some are more basic than others (would I ever be caught dead in Uggs? No. A polyester flower crown from the Forever 21 sale bin? Well, maybe . . .), I do relish life's most simple pleasures, such as imbibing bottomless mimosas, lighting a Farmer's Market–scented Yankee Candle, and eating avocado toast on flaxseed-heavy bread. And that's entirely okay! Life is complex. Humans are complex. There should be zero shame in celebrating the most basic clothing, food, drinks, and activities that give us this reliable pleasure.

Perhaps the biggest misconception about being a basic bitch is that we lack sophistication or the desire to seek experiences that challenge our basicness. This could not be further from the truth—for me, at least. In fact, I am so obsessed with traveling the world, trying different foods, and learning new things that being basic is my respite from the exhaustion and chaos of everyday life. I look forward to the moments when I can mindlessly binge-watch *Friends* while chugging rosé out of an oversize wineglass. I crave the cooler months when I can stroll through Central Park in comfy flannel and suede Chelsea boots. It's my basicness that grounds me and, like my unapologetic ritual of starting to play Christmas music in July, prevents me from grabbing a bottle of Xanax or texting an ex-boyfriend as a way to distract myself from my damn-near-impossible to-do lists.

When it comes to food, specifically, there are plenty of meals associated with the basic bitch lifestyle. Loved ones can't seem to grasp how I partake in $300 dinners with exotic proteins and hard-to-pronounce sauces, only to wake up and crave a simple peanut-butter-and-jelly sandwich. My response? Hi, I have these things called taste buds, and peanut butter is and always will be effing amazing (seriously, if you don't like peanut butter and/or lack a desire to eat it straight from the jar, this raises some major concerns). You *can* have your flourless chocolate cake (page 162) and eat it too. Plus, many basic bitch dishes capitalize on health trends and superfoods, so they boast things such as fiber and collagen that ultimately make you feel good, or at least trick you into thinking you do. You'd think it's like, science or something.

My relationship with cooking basic cuisine started when I was in middle school. It was an easy way to harness my control-freak tendencies (yay for steps and precise measurements!) and concoct meals that were small on difficulty but big on bold, satisfying flavors. This usually came in the form of pasta or ground turkey with excessive amounts of herbs, spices, and cheeses added. Gourmet? Far from it, but I was so impressed with my ability to whip up an uncomplicated, delicious dish that I would challenge my family members to do better. This ultimately resulted in *Iron Chef*–style battles where we'd scour the internet for recipes and duke it out for temporary bragging rights. To this day, we still attack Thanksgiving and Christmas with the same competitive spirit, and I may or may not still cry if I lose.

Through these culinary journeys, I've also found that the best recipes are those that are effortless, inspirational over aspirational, and, most important, dependable. I want friends and family to feel they can revisit, revise, and reimagine these tastes without having to invest in a cooking class or ridiculously expensive supplies. I also hope they can relive some of the familiar flavors of their youth, since it's okay to crave that spinach-and-artichoke dip (page 48) you ate daily in high school or that açaí bowl (page 185) you can't stop thinking about from that super-trendy health store in Beverly Hills. Just because #TBT cuisine has become ingrained in our day-to-day culture (and almost comically so) doesn't mean it is any less appetizing. There's a reason dishes develop cult followings: People know exactly what they want, when they want it, and they'll do whatever it takes to satisfy that craving. Make the damn dip or açai bowl, smile adorably once you've mastered it, and enjoy it . . . perhaps behind closed doors, because you know the double chin–inducing faces you make when something is *that good*.

So whether you're an awful cook, a recent grad, or someone who just enjoys their meals basic, the purpose of this book is to arm you with over one hundred tried-and-true recipes that are not only delicious but super easy to make. You'll also learn some things along the way, such as pantry necessities, cooking tips and tricks, and how to shop at a farmers' market (no, I don't rely just on my Yankee Candle for these wonderful smells). You don't have to become the next Ina Garten (though she's fabulous and a true representation of basic bitch in peak form), but I do hope you'll feel confident enough to embrace the basic bitch lifestyle and use it to create some marvelous and memorable dishes. Basic foods are always the biggest crowd-pleasers, after all.

Now is the time to pop that collar, water that dying succulent in your kitchen, and restock your Khloé Kardashian–inspired storage bins. If you chop garlic like you're hammering together an IKEA dresser, fine. You're not here for anyone else's judgment . . . except maybe your own, like the true basic bitch that you are.

ALONG THE WAY I OFFER GUIDANCE FOR EACH RECIPE:

Just the Tips: Tips, tricks, advice, and suggestions

The More You Glow: Health benefits and nutritional breakdowns

Literally Can't Even: Substitutions, variations, and additions

Basic Basics: Mini recipes and ingredient/dish explainers

How to Stock a Basic Pantry

Congratulations! You probably have the internet and can order any ingredient at any time to be delivered within any two-hour window (#technology). But there are a handful of pantry staples that are worth stocking up on, if only to satisfy those two a.m. cravings when you decide to host a *MasterChef* competition against your drunk alter ego, Helga, who is demanding delicious food and demanding it quick. These are the versatile ingredients you'll tend to use most often in the kitchen, which means you'll now have another excuse to make that Costco trip you so desperately want to make but so desperately don't really need to.

THE *basic* BITCHEN PANTRY ESSENTIALS

BAKING SODA AND BAKING POWDER

A necessary duo for any type of baking and the only white powder, aside from flour, that should be anywhere near your home. What did D.A.R.E. and your early twenties teach you, after all?

BEANS (CANNED OR DRY)

They're not good just for your heart. The more you eat, the more you . . . up your protein intake and avoid certain digestive activities that basic bitches don't engage in.

BROTH OR STOCK

You'll be armed and ready to make every soup and stew you can imagine. So what are you waiting for, Brad Pitt to fall in love with you? Ain't happenin', but soup and stew will.

CANNED TOMATOES

All about that base, 'bout that base—base for so much more than the marinara you're going to dump all over pasta and pile high with grated cheese. Canned tomatoes lend themselves to a slew of slow cooker meals such as tikka masala, Thai chicken curry, and game-day (lol, as if you actually care about sports) chili.

FLOUR

Don't expect to make cookies, cakes, and pies without it, which means you also shouldn't expect to wean yourself from those happy pills without it.

GARLIC

My body is approximately 5 percent garlic, so you'd be wrong to tell me that the powerful root isn't a necessary part of anyone's daily diet. Not only is it one of the best superfoods on earth, but its sharp flavor can breathe life into any dish and breathe death into your breath.

HOT SAUCE

I got it in my bag and not just because I emulate Beyoncé on a regular basis. Whether it's sriracha, aged chili, or fiery habanero, hot sauce will enhance the flavor of anything you're adding it to, making it a pantry must-have for leftovers, international dishes, or your boyfriend's notoriously bland cooking.

MUSTARD

The Adriana Lima of condiments: perfect in every way. Mustard, particularly a good Dijon, is the foundation of many sauces, dressings, and vinaigrettes. It's also fantastic on its own, which means you can dip and dunk your way through a meal of tangy bliss.

NUTS AND NUT BUTTER

Nuts: great for snacking on and kicking when men disappoint you. Nut butter: great for spreading on bread for a meal that never fails to satisfy, unlike men . . . who are disappointing.

OATS

They may be a shabby shade of beige, but you'll never be short on breakfast in the form of oatmeal, granola, and overnight oats.

OILS

I always opt for an extra-virgin olive oil, but canola is pretty standard across cooking and baking. And it's also cheap, much like the hair dryer I just bought that shoots sparks directly into my hair. (That's its way of saying, "Baby, you're a firework," or so I've convinced myself in an effort to distract from the real possibility of my head catching on fire.)

ONIONS

Sure, they'll make you cry more than *A Walk to Remember*, but I haven't really found a savory dish where onions can't be added. As with polishes at a nail salon, there are so many to choose from and there's a time and purpose for each of them. Onions are a great way to impart wonderfully unique flavors into sauces, marinades, proteins, and pizzas, so don't be shy. That's why breath mints were invented.

PASTA

Affordable, long-lasting, the food BFF that never lets you down. She comes in all shapes and sizes and we accept her unconditionally . . . even if she *is* a carb.

RICE

Perhaps the most internationally adored and utilized ingredient of all time, rice has a shelf life that far exceeds your Botox injections.

SPICES AND SEASONINGS

If you don't cook with salt, you don't cook with love. And if you don't cook with love, then don't expect to find a husband. (Kidding, kind of.) Spices and seasonings, which can include peppers, dried herbs, and more exotic blends of ingredients, are essential for turning any dish from drab to fab. If only you could sprinkle some on last year's weathered wardrobe and get the same effect.

SUGAR

This one's pretty self-explanatory. Sure, you can use substitutes such as honey or even agave nectar in many cases, but nothing rivals America's favorite crop and the reason you don't want to rock that crop top.

TUNA FISH

Some may consider this a last resort, but canned tuna is easy enough to doctor and make appetizing when you're suffering from one of the following: a weeping bank account, pure and utter laziness, or an intense desire for quick protein that isn't a processed meat.

VANILLA EXTRACT

Being vanilla is finally a good thing! Avoid imitation at all costs, and enjoy the depth of flavor this liquid addition will bring to all your baked goods.

VINEGARS

Balsamic is boss, but a lighter variety such as apple cider vinegar or rice vinegar is more versatile across most recipes. Honestly, you can't have enough vinegar, so buy every type, try them all, and take shots of whatever you don't enjoy because it's *that* healthy for you. Or at least a much healthier alternative to vodka.

Kitchen Tool Basics

Whether you've just moved into a new home, are looking to impress future in-laws, or simply want to channel your inner amateur chef, you're going to rely on a few cooking tools to make your life a helluva lot easier in the kitchen. This comprehensive list lays out everything you need, everything you might need, and everything you need to add to this year's holiday wish list, because cabinet and drawer space is tight, Mama's on a budget, and some things are nothing but a luxury (looking at you, salad spinner).

THE *basic* BITCHEN ESSENTIALS

BAKING OR CASSEROLE DISH
Scoopable meals rely on this one. And a scoopable meal usually means a delicious meal.

BAKING SHEET
The largest you can get. Nobody bakes fewer than a dozen cookies. And if they do, we don't like them.

BOWLS
Because mixing in that empty lavender-scented laundry detergent tub is probably not your safest or most palatable option.

CAN OPENER
If you want to rely on the ol' pocketknife trick, good luck to you and the hand that will most likely put you in the emergency room.

CHEF'S KNIFE
To slice, dice, mince, chop, julienne, and every other verb associated with a sharp object. Please exercise caution around manicured hands and cheating ex-boyfriends.

COLANDER
The only thing worth straining is pasta on a Friday night.

CUTTING BOARD
Get yourself a sturdy wooden board to protect your granite countertop and, ultimately, the resale value of your home (or, let's be honest, the full amount of your security deposit, for most of us). Opt for a plastic, dishwasher-safe one to use for raw proteins such as chicken.

GLASSES (DRINKING, WINE, AND CHAMPAGNE FLUTES)
Drinking from the blender, shaker, or even bottle sure is tempting, but we're sophisticated bitches.

LADLE
Try scooping hot liquid with a spatula and see how that fares. Never a good time.

LOAF PAN
Your bake-sale breads will never look more carbolicious.

MEASURING CUPS (DRY AND LIQUID)
No need to go up a cup size. Embrace exactly what God, err, the recipe gave you for failproof results. Use a glass measuring cup (the kind with a spout) for liquids and dry measuring cups (the kind that usually come in a set with ¼, ⅓, ½, and 1 cup options) for dry ingredients.

MEASURING SPOONS
Baking is all about precision. Don't trust your eyes or your hands—you've seen how you hold a mascara wand.

MUFFIN PAN
No, not the Muffin Man. Though we sure wish he was included with purchase, sans muffin top and full of rock-hard abs.

PAN/SKILLET SET
Unless you plan to cook your food over coals or a flat iron, you'll need a nice pan/skillet set. Nonstick is the best for that egg white omelet in the a.m.

PIE PLATE/PAN
Don't expect to win any county fair competitions without it.

ROUND CAKE PANS
You'll need two if you want a layer cake (or two separate cakes because it's just been one of those weeks).

SAUCEPAN SET OR A GOOD DUTCH OVEN
For steaming, boiling, and tossing everything that's about to go bad in your fridge while crossing your fingers and praying for a dinnertime miracle.

SPATULA
You'll need this to mix your dishes; mix them real good. Ooh, baby, baby.

WINE OPENER OR CORKSCREW
If you're not drinking wine while cooking, you're not doing it right.

REALLY *nice* TO HAVE

COCKTAIL SHAKER
The Shake Weight is so 2009. Get your Michelle Obama biceps by prepping for happy hour.

JIGGER
Stop blaming that battery-acid-levels-of-nasty cocktail on a *heavy hand*. We're officially above eyeballing.

KITCHEN SHEARS
Because those fatty chicken breasts aren't going on the South Beach Diet to defat themselves.

MICROPLANE
Your zesty bestie for any citrus rind. Also great for garlic and ginger, the two Gs found in every drool-worthy Asian recipe.

ROLLING PIN
Honestly, these are just fun to use and always guarantee dough precision. Note to my fellow Italians who misbehaved as children: This may trigger some PTSD.

SPOONS (STIRRING, WOODEN, SLOTTED)
Spatula reinforcements that can also cling to brownie batter and cookie dough, aka the only reasons you're making dessert to begin with.

THERMOMETER
To determine if something isn't just, like, kind of hot, but, like, hot hot.

TONGS
Homemade chicken fingers can't be made without them. The same goes for anything that requires a good flip or dip on the stove or in the oven.

WHISK
A fork will work in most situations, but who needs the wrist wrinkles?

SO *extra*, BUT SO WORTH IT

APRON
A basic bitch always dresses the part.

CAST-IRON SKILLET
Don't be afraid. When it comes to maintenance, it's not even half as difficult as the SATs.

FINE-MESH SIEVE
Perhaps the easiest way to make something thinner. Unfortunately, we can't jump through one ourselves. Also ideal for sifting.

GRATER
Step away from the charcuterie board and grate your remaining hard blocks. Your nutritionist will thank you.

GRILL PAN
I'll take sear marks over stretch marks any day.

ICE CREAM SCOOP
Rarely used for ice cream, ironically, but you can bank on perfectly symmetrical cookies to ease your OCD.

LEMON SQUEEZER
Easy-peasy, lemon squeezy, minus the seeds and with even more juice.

OTHER KNIVES (BREAD, PARING, AND THE LIKE)
Honestly, a knife block will do the trick. No need to overthink this like everything else in your life.

OVEN MITTS
Oven mitts are cuter (and safer!) than moldy dishrags.

PASTRY BRUSH
Take that pastry to the Salon of Basic and give her a nice gloss and color, girl. Yaaas.

SALAD SPINNER
Dry lettuce is good lettuce. Wilted lettuce is lettuce that goes directly into the trash, along with broken hair ties, empty Pringles cans, and men who catcall you on the street.

SPLATTER GUARD
Why would you want to ruin the apron that is protecting the $5 shirt you'd cry about staining? A splatter guard is also a great safety precaution against burns (but not the verbal ones from your mother).

TRIVET
That Crate & Barrel dining table is far cuter without a circle scorched on it.

VEGETABLE PEELER
Like a therapist or pint of cookie dough ice cream: there to make your life easier.

Basic Bevs

Aside from crafting, organizing, complaining, cozying up to a pet or nonexistent boyfriend, and snacking while watching Netflix, there's nothing a basic bitch loves more than sipping.

The simple action, whether through a straw, delicately from a mug, or sloppily from a Solo cup, can yield a world of possibilities: hydration, sustenance, relaxation, stimulation, and, perhaps our favorite state, drunkenness. But the liquid game is constantly evolving. While basic bitch staples such as pumpkin spice lattes and rosé certainly aren't going anywhere anytime soon, they're now adorned with edible flowers and the like, infused with trendy herbal tinctures, or reimagined with different colors, ingredients, and preparations. And I'm here for it.

This bevy of bevs, ranging from familiar to trendy, healthy to alcoholic, is a basic bitch mealtime necessity. They're also the perfect drinks for after-work happy hours, spontaneous cocktail soirees, and preplanned gatherings, such as sorority retreats or Rodan + Fields "parties." So raise your glass to a new catalog of delicious offerings that you can now cheers with your favorite gays and girlfriends.

1

Basic Bitch Lifeblood, aka the Pumpkin Spice Latte

PREP TIME: 5 MINUTES **COOK TIME:** 5 MINUTES
TOTAL TIME: 10 MINUTES **YIELD:** 2 DRINKS

On a scale of one to "I want to punch you in the face," I'm practically a broken jaw when it comes to how annoying I am about the arrival of fall. And nothing screams "fall" more than a pumpkin spice latte, despite the fact that its annual debut happens before we even have the chance to wipe off the sunscreen and dust off our old Uggs. Sure, that smirking green siren may make a decent one (she's trademarked the term "PSL," after all), but this homemade alternative with actual pumpkin puree will knock your *hygge*-friendly wool socks off. In fact, if you make it and aren't 100 percent satisfied, then you're definitely not the type to know where your locally sourced kale comes from, and I simply can't relate.

1 First make the pumpkin spice blend: In a medium bowl, whisk the cinnamon, ginger, nutmeg, allspice, and cloves until combined. Transfer to an airtight container and set aside.

2 Next make the sweetened whipped cream: In a large bowl, whisk the cream, confectioners' sugar, and vanilla until the cream holds soft peaks. Keep chilled until ready to use.

3 Make the lattes: In a small saucepan over medium heat, combine the pumpkin puree, ½ teaspoon of the pumpkin spice blend, and granulated sugar. Cook, stirring constantly, until heated through, about 2 minutes. Whisk in the vanilla and milk until fully combined and hot. Remove from the heat and transfer to a blender. Blend until frothed, 1 to 2 minutes.

4 Divide the espresso between two coffee mugs and add the frothed pumpkin mixture. If desired, top with a dollop of sweetened whipped cream and garnish with a sprinkle of additional pumpkin spice blend. Serve immediately.

LITERALLY CAN'T EVEN

Whole milk is best, but you can use 2% or skim.

Use your favorite sugar replacement instead of granulated sugar, to taste.

Feeling adventurous? Roast off a pumpkin and put it in the food processor to make your own puree instead of buying canned pumpkin (see page 168).

FOR THE PUMPKIN SPICE BLEND
3 tablespoons ground cinnamon
2 teaspoons ground ginger
2 teaspoons ground nutmeg
1¼ teaspoons ground allspice
1¼ teaspoons ground cloves

FOR THE SWEETENED WHIPPED CREAM
½ cup heavy cream, chilled
1 tablespoon confectioners' sugar
¼ teaspoon vanilla extract

FOR THE LATTES
2 tablespoons pure pumpkin puree
3 tablespoons granulated sugar
1 tablespoon vanilla extract
2 cups whole milk
¼ to ⅓ cup freshly brewed espresso

JUST THE TIPS

While you can use store-bought pumpkin spice, it's best to make your own, which can last up to 6 months in an airtight container.

Just because it's a warm fall day doesn't mean you can't have your pumpkin spice latte—make it iced! Simply cool your ingredients before adding a cup of ice for a chilled pumpkin spice latte. You can make your espresso ahead of time and keep it in the refrigerator for a pumpkin spice latte on the go.

Give Me Angelina Jolie's Collarbones Detox Smoothie

PREP TIME: 5 MINUTES **TOTAL TIME:** 5 MINUTES **YIELD:** 2 DRINKS

1 cup coconut water, plus more as needed

¹/₂ cup fresh carrot juice

1 banana, frozen

1 cup frozen pineapple chunks

1 cup baby spinach

1 small red beet, peeled and small diced

2 tablespoons freshly squeezed lemon juice (from 1 medium lemon)

1 (¹/₂-inch) piece fresh turmeric, peeled

1 (¹/₂-inch) piece fresh ginger, peeled

1¹/₂ teaspoons moringa powder

Pinch of cayenne pepper

¹/₂ cup ice

A bitter-tasting smoothie is more annoying than someone who puts an apostrophe when trying (and failing) to make a word plural. Trendy ingredients such as moringa, spirulina, and balboa are hard to say and even harder to mask in a postworkout bev. They don't taste good on their own and, when combined, can emit smells that rival my third-grade teacher's halitosis. Until now. Somehow, I've managed to concoct a blend that doesn't smell like a subway platform as you sip. And it's chock-full of all the vitamins, nutrients, and minerals that dietitians say are good for you. You're welcome, health freaks.

In a blender, combine the coconut water, carrot juice, banana, pineapple, spinach, beet, lemon juice, turmeric, ginger, moringa powder, cayenne, and ice. Blend on high until smooth and thick. Divide between two glasses and serve immediately.

JUST THE TIPS
Be careful of the yellow stains turmeric leaves on everything, including your hands.

THE MORE YOU GLOW

- **Coconut Water:** Low in calories and carbohydrates. Rich in electrolytes. Great source of hydration.

- **Spinach:** Loaded with iron, calcium, potassium, and magnesium; vitamins A, C, and K_1; folic acid; and omega-3 fatty acids. Good source of fiber.

- **Beets:** Full of iron, vitamin C, fiber, magnesium, and potassium.

- **Lemons:** High in vitamins C and B. Citric acid helps with digestion. Low in sugar. Skin brightener.

- **Cayenne:** Immune booster; may increase metabolism (increases heat in the body, making you burn more calories).

- **Moringa:** Leaves are rich in protein, vitamins B_6 and C, riboflavin, and iron. Can reduce blood sugar and inflammation.

- **Turmeric:** Anti-inflammatory (because of curcumin, the active ingredient in turmeric). Increases antioxidants in the body.

- **Ginger:** Related to turmeric; powerful anti-inflammatory and antioxidant effects. Can help soothe nausea/stomachaches, ease muscle pain/soreness, and reduce indigestion.

- **Carrots:** Good source of beta-carotene, fiber, vitamins (K_1, biotin, A, and B_6), potassium, and antioxidants. Pectin is the main source of soluble fiber in carrots.

- **Banana:** Digestion aid; high in potassium.

- **Pineapple:** High in vitamin C; anti-inflammatory; digestive aid.

Shantay, You Frosé

PREP TIME: 5 MINUTES **COOK TIME:** 5 MINUTES
TOTAL TIME: 5 HOURS 10 MINUTES **YIELD:** 4 DRINKS

Frosé on a summer day is more satisfying than a childhood bully growing up to be ugly. Normal liquid rosé is already a fabulous complement to brunch foods and petty conversation, but we basics like it frozen, not unlike our foreheads after a semiannual tune-up with injectables. This is why frosé is basicness at its peak. It's refreshing, it's pink, it's sweet, it gets you drunk, it's Insta-ready, and it's surprisingly easy to make on your own. Just use the entire bottle and invite some friends over to lip-synch for their lives. I judge anyone who needs to invest in a wine stopper.

---

1 First make the simple syrup: In a small pot, combine the water and sugar and bring to a boil. Stir until the sugar dissolves; remove from the heat. Let cool to room temperature, transfer to an airtight container, and refrigerate for up to 2 weeks.

2 Pour the rosé into a zip-top bag. Seal the bag and lay it flat in a baking dish. Freeze for a minimum of 5 hours.

3 In a blender, combine the frozen rosé, strawberries, lemon juice, and ¼ cup of the simple syrup. Blend until a slushy consistency is reached. Pour into glasses and serve, garnished with mint and a tropical drink umbrella.

LITERALLY CAN'T EVEN

A classic frosé uses simple syrup to sweeten the drink. If you aren't a fan of refined sugars, substitute honey, agave nectar, or maple syrup.

Traditionally, frosé is made with strawberries, but feel free to make it your own. A mixture of strawberry and watermelon, mango and peach, or strawberry and raspberry are all great options.

You can customize your simple syrups to include different flavors—for example, herbs, citrus, spices, dried chilies, and so forth. Don't be afraid to experiment. Just add your aromatics when you remove the simple syrup from the heat.

FOR THE SIMPLE SYRUP

1 cup water

1 cup sugar

1 (750-milliliter) bottle rosé wine

8 ounces (1½ cups) fresh strawberries, frozen

¼ cup freshly squeezed lemon juice (from 2 medium lemons)

Mint, for garnish

JUST THE TIPS

Pour a little chilled rosé over your frosé before serving.

Don't water down your frosé with extra ice; instead, freeze your rosé and fruit. Rosé can be frozen up to a week in advance.

Freezing rosé results in the loss of some of its pink color, so make sure to choose a rosé with a deeper pink hue.

Feeling wild? Kick it up a notch by adding ½ cup vodka before blending or as a floater!

Vodka & Me: A Love Story

Shout-out to my number one girl, vodka, and the many ways in which we can consume her. After a few of the drinks on the following pages, your only concern will be why Tyra Banks's "Shake Your Body" or the soundtrack to *Thumbelina* still isn't on Spotify. From a simple vodka soda to a classic dirty martini, this beautifully boozy assortment has you covered. I've also thrown in a cosmo because Carrie Bradshaw is #goals when it comes to life in NYC. My dreams of meeting a Wall Street man, not boy, who buys us a penthouse apartment while I continue to use my rent-controlled studio as a "writer's loft" *will* happen . . . with the help of vodka, of course. Delusion is a cute look.

Vodka Soda: "The Little Black Dress of Cocktails"

PREP TIME: 1 MINUTE   **TOTAL TIME:** 1 MINUTE   **YIELD:** 1 DRINK

Fill a glass with ice and pour the vodka over the top. Top with a squeeze of lime juice and the club soda. Garnish with a lime wedge and serve.

Ice cubes
2 ounces vodka, chilled
Squeeze of lime juice
6 ounces club soda
Lime wedge, for garnish

JUST THE TIPS

Always keep your vodka in the freezer. The colder the cocktail, the better.

Use large ice cubes. No crushed ice here.

Make sure your club soda is freshly opened and super-carbonated. Don't grab an old bottle from the back of the fridge.

Always use fresh lime juice (from a lime, not from a bottle!)—same goes for lemon juice.

LITERALLY CAN'T EVEN

If the club soda isn't doing it for you, swap in your favorite diet cola.

Ice cubes

2 ounces vodka, chilled

1 ounce cranberry juice cocktail

1¹/₂ ounces freshly squeezed lime juice (from 1¹/₂ limes)

³/₄ ounce orange liqueur

Orange twist, for garnish

JUST THE TIPS

Your cosmopolitan should be a pale pink color. You want to balance the sweetness of the cranberry juice cocktail with the tartness of the lime juice.

When shaking your cocktail, make sure to do so for at least 30 seconds, until the shaker is frosted and the drink is cold.

The glass matters. Always serve your cosmo in a chilled martini glass.

Ice cubes

2¹/₂ ounces vodka, chilled

¹/₄ ounce dry vermouth

¹/₂ ounce olive juice (from a jar of olives), or to taste

Pimiento-stuffed green olives, for garnish

JUST THE TIPS

"Dirty" refers to the addition of olive juice. A "filthy" martini has extra olive juice added.

Stir the ingredients together; do not shake them—that will dilute the flavor.

Always serve in a chilled martini glass.

Cosmopolitan

PREP TIME: 3 MINUTES   **TOTAL TIME:** 3 MINUTES   **YIELD:** 1 DRINK

1   Chill a martini glass.

2   Fill a cocktail shaker with ice and add the vodka, cranberry juice cocktail, lime juice, and orange liqueur. Shake vigorously until well chilled, about 30 seconds. Strain into the chilled martini glass and garnish with the orange twist. Serve immediately.

LITERALLY CAN'T EVEN

If you opt to use unsweetened cranberry juice instead of cranberry juice cocktail, the drink may be too tart. Balance it out with a little agave nectar or simple syrup (see page 15).

Dirty Martini

PREP TIME: 1 MINUTE   **TOTAL TIME:** 1 MINUTE   **YIELD:** 1 DRINK

1   Chill a martini glass.

2   Fill a cocktail shaker with ice, add the vodka, vermouth, and olive juice, and stir. Strain into the chilled martini glass. Garnish with olives and serve.

LITERALLY CAN'T EVEN

Not craving the vodka? (Gasp!) Switch it up by making a gin martini instead.

Feeling fancy? Serve with blue cheese–stuffed olives.

Orange Cream Gelatin Shots

PREP TIME: 5 MINUTES   **COOK TIME:** 5 MINUTES
TOTAL TIME: 2 HOURS 10 MINUTES   **YIELD:** 16 (1-OUNCE) SHOTS

4 ounces whipped cream–
flavored vodka

1 ounce orange liqueur

1 ounce freshly squeezed
orange juice

¹/₄ cup cold water

1 (3-ounce) box orange gelatin

1 cup boiling water

Whipped cream, for serving
(optional)

1   In a 2-cup measuring cup, combine the vodka, orange liqueur, orange juice, and cold water. Set in the fridge to chill while you prepare the remaining ingredients.

2   Put the gelatin in a medium bowl. Pour the boiling water over the gelatin and stir until it is completely dissolved, about 2 minutes. Stir in the chilled vodka mixture until combined. Pour into shot glasses and refrigerate until set, at least 2 hours or up to overnight. Serve chilled, topped with whipped cream, if desired.

LITERALLY CAN'T EVEN
Switch up the flavor of the gelatin and juices to make all kinds of different combinations. Just make sure that you stick to the basic ratios so the gelatin sets: 1 cup boiling water, 1 (3-ounce) package gelatin, 5 to 6 ounces liquor, and ¹/₄ cup cold water.

Celebrity Celery Celebration Green Juice

PREP TIME: 15 MINUTES   **TOTAL TIME:** 15 MINUTES   **YIELD:** 4 DRINKS

FOR THE CELERY JUICE
1 bunch celery, ends trimmed, cut into thirds

1/4 cup water

FOR THE GREEN JUICE
1 cup baby spinach

1 green apple, cored and quartered

1/2 cup freshly squeezed lemon juice (from 3 medium lemons)

1 (1-inch) piece fresh ginger, peeled

1 English cucumber, quartered

1 cup fresh flat-leaf parsley

JUST THE TIPS
It's ideal to make a green juice in a juicer, but if you don't have one on hand, you can use a high-speed blender.

LITERALLY CAN'T EVEN
Kick your green juice up a notch by adding a shot of wheatgrass.

There's something extremely off-putting about drinking your vegetables, but anything that touts unscientifically proven results of getting skinny makes it worth trying, right? And no, I don't need Kylie Jenner's approval (even though I really want it). In all honesty, I'm happy the juice cleanse fad has been reined in and we can use drinks like these to supplement our diets and make us feel good. I like to guzzle this right when I wake up on an empty stomach, because it activates my intestines into doing things we classy ladies like to pretend we never, ever do.

1   First make the celery juice: In a blender, combine the celery and water. Blend on high until smooth. Strain through cheesecloth into a bowl, squeezing the cheesecloth to extract all the juice. Discard the celery pulp. Transfer to an airtight jar and refrigerate until cold or up to 24 hours.

2   Next make the green juice: Place 1½ cups of the celery juice, the spinach, apple, lemon juice, ginger, cucumber, and parsley in a blender and blend until smooth. Strain through cheesecloth into a pitcher, squeezing the cheesecloth to extract all the juice. Discard the pulp. Transfer to the fridge to chill.

3   When ready to serve, pour into four glasses and serve immediately.

THE MORE YOU GLOW
- Wheatgrass: High in vitamins A, C, and E; iron, magnesium, and calcium; and eight essential amino acids. Can alleviate inflammation.

- Celery juice: Powerful antioxidant properties. Phytochemicals in celery help to reduce blood pressure, reduce inflammation, and fight oxidative stress. Rich in vitamins A, C, and K; folic acid; the essential electrolytes calcium, potassium, sodium, magnesium, and phosphorus; and smaller amounts of other vitamins and minerals.

Pinot Grigi-OMG Yes, Sangria

PREP TIME: 10 MINUTES   **TOTAL TIME:** 3 HOURS 10 MINUTES
YIELD: 8 DRINKS

There have been plenty of times when I have forgotten to bring my lunch to work but remembered to bring a bottle of wine for after-work happy hour. As I see it, this doesn't mean I'm irresponsible, just someone who truly understands life's priorities. If that day happens to be in the summer, the bottle is usually pinot grigio or Sancerre. And since I carry these bottles by the dozen, an ideal way to zhuzh 'em up is to transform this sometimes mediocre white wine into a refreshing golden sangria. The key to this recipe is customization. Whether it's berries, stone fruits, or a citrusy Grand Marnier, you get to call the shots (literally) and create a sipper that is reflective of both your unique tastes and your unique personality.

In a large pitcher, combine the apple brandy, lime, lemon, green apple, strawberries, and sugar, mashing gently to release the juices from the fruit. Pour the pinot grigio over the fruit and stir to combine. Cover and transfer to the refrigerator to chill for at least 3 hours or up to overnight. Remove from the refrigerator, pour into glasses, and top with club soda. Garnish with mint and serve.

LITERALLY CAN'T EVEN

Wine and fruit juices are great, but we're looking for a bit more pizzazz with this cocktail. Spike it with some high-proof spirits—for example, Grand Marnier, Cointreau, triple sec, brandy, and the like.

Bubbles are a fabulous addition to keep this drink light for the summertime.

---

2 ounces apple brandy

1 lime, sliced

1 lemon, sliced

1 green apple, cored and sliced

1 cup strawberries, sliced

3 tablespoons sugar

1 (750-milliliter) bottle pinot grigio

8 ounces club soda

Mint, for garnish

JUST THE TIPS

Now is not the time to break out the $60 bottle of pinot grigio. Use inexpensive wine when making a mixed cocktail, but not *cheap* wine. It should still be a wine you'd love to drink on its own.

Don't just cut up the fruits. Make sure to mash them to release the juices into the sangria.

Matcha Latta, Ya Ya

PREP TIME: 5 MINUTES   **COOK TIME:** 5 MINUTES
TOTAL TIME: 10 MINUTES   **YIELD:** 1 DRINK

¹/₄ cup hot (not boiling) water
1 teaspoon matcha powder
1 cup oat milk
5 drops liquid stevia
¹/₄ teaspoon ground cinnamon
2 scoops collagen peptides

LITERALLY CAN'T EVEN

Adjust the sweetness based on your preference. You can substitute agave nectar, maple syrup, coconut sugar, honey, raw sugar, or any other sweetener.

The only bags I want anywhere near my eyes are Chanel, and because I don't typically drink coffee, matcha is my go-to for a quick caffeine fix. There's something about the electric-green tea that gives you a healthy zing and not the standing-in-line-for-a-Celine-Dion-concert jitters I get with coffee. It's also jam-packed with antioxidants and delicious without added sugars or sucralose. "So why don't you marry it?"—stereotypical bully on the playground. At this rate, anything is possible, including a matcha cocktail that I threw in for the girl who means business but is all about the party.

1   Combine the hot water and matcha powder in a mug and let sit for 1 to 2 minutes, whisking to break up any clumps of matcha. If you do not have a matcha whisk, a regular small whisk will do just fine.

2   In a small saucepan, combine the oat milk, matcha mixture, stevia, and cinnamon. Cook over medium heat, whisking constantly, until small bubbles appear. Remove from the heat and transfer to a blender. Add the collagen. Blend on high until foam appears. Pour the matcha latte into a mug and serve.

THE MORE YOU GLOW

- Matcha: Contains the nutrients from the entire tea leaf, making it higher in caffeine and antioxidants than traditional green tea. Boosts metabolism and burns calories. Contains vitamin C, selenium, chromium, zinc, and magnesium.

- Collagen peptides: Helps improve hair, skin, nails, joints and ligaments, and tendon health. Packs 18 grams of protein in 2 scoops—and only 70 calories! Free of gluten, dairy, and sugar.

- Stevia: A very sweet plant, part of the sunflower family, used to sweeten beverages and meals. Can be classified as "zero-calorie." It is two hundred to three hundred times sweeter than table sugar.

- Oat milk: Good nondairy alternative for people with allergies or intolerances. It's free of lactose, nuts, soy, and gluten. Vegan-friendly.

Matcha Cocktail

PREP TIME: 5 MINUTES **COOK TIME:** 5 MINUTES
TOTAL TIME: 10 MINUTES PLUS COOLING **YIELD:** 1 DRINK

1 First make the basil simple syrup: In a small saucepot, combine the water and sugar and bring to a boil. Stir until the sugar dissolves and then remove from the heat. Add the basil and let cool to room temperature. Remove the basil and transfer the simple syrup to an airtight container. Store in the fridge for up to 2 weeks.

2 In a cocktail shaker filled with ice, combine the gin, lemon juice, matcha powder, and 2 tablespoons of the basil simple syrup. Shake vigorously for 1 minute, until well chilled. Strain into a glass filled with ice and top with club soda. Garnish with a cucumber ribbon and basil sprig and serve.

FOR THE BASIL
SIMPLE SYRUP
$^1/_2$ cup water
$^1/_2$ cup sugar
3 basil sprigs

Ice cubes
2 ounces gin
1 ounce freshly squeezed lemon juice (from 1 medium lemon)
1 teaspoon matcha powder
Club soda, to top
Cucumber ribbon, for garnish
Basil sprig, for garnish

You're So Vanilla Milkshake

PREP TIME: 5 MINUTES **TOTAL TIME:** 5 MINUTES **YIELD:** 1 DRINK

1 cup vanilla ice cream, softened

¹/₂ teaspoon vanilla bean paste

¹/₂ cup whole milk or nut milk (see page 29)

Whipped cream, for garnish

Maraschino cherry, for garnish

You may not be bringing all the boys to the yard, but you'll certainly be bringing them to your kitchen with this easily customizable take on an American classic. Since nut milks from literally every type of nut are all the rage, there's also a world of healthy possibilities and more combinations than Cher's closet in *Clueless*. You probably won't be wearing an Alaïa anytime soon, but after occasionally subbing nut milk for dairy, you'll at least be able to fit in one and avoid being a virgin who can't drive.

JUST THE TIPS

Always chill the glass your milkshake is going into.

Make sure your ice cream is soft but not runny. If the ice cream is too hard, you will add too much milk, diluting the milkshake.

Don't use ice in your milkshake—it will only water down the finished product!

1 Place a pint glass in the freezer to chill.

2 In a blender, combine the ice cream, vanilla bean paste, and milk. Blend on high until smooth. Pour into the chilled pint glass and top with whipped cream and a cherry. Serve with a straw.

LITERALLY CAN'T EVEN

The perfect milkshake is very personal. If you like your milkshake thicker, cut back on the liquid; if you like it thinner, feel free to add a bit more.

Not into ice cream? Substitute frozen yogurt.

Going dairy-free? Use dairy-free vanilla ice cream and any dairy-free milk and omit the whipped cream.

Interested in making a grown-up milkshake? Add a splash of your favorite booze!

Nut Milk

PREP TIME: 5 MINUTES **COOK TIME:** 5 MINUTES
TOTAL TIME: 10 MINUTES PLUS SOAKING **YIELD:** 4 CUPS

1 Put the nuts in a medium bowl and cover with about 2 inches of water. Cover the bowl with plastic wrap and transfer to the refrigerator to soak for at least 12 hours or up to 2 days. The nuts will plump and soften the longer they sit. For a creamier milk, let the nuts soak for a longer amount of time.

2 Drain and rinse the nuts and transfer them to a blender. Add the hot water, salt, and honey, if using. Blend on high speed for about 3 minutes. Line a colander with cheesecloth and set it over a large bowl. Strain the nut milk through the cheesecloth, pressing on the solids to release all the liquid. Discard the nut pulp or reserve for future use. Transfer the nut milk to an airtight container and refrigerate until ready to use, up to three days.

1 cup raw nuts (cashews, almonds, pistachios, hazelnuts, pecans, walnuts, peanuts, or any others)

3 cups hot water

$1/4$ teaspoon kosher salt

1 tablespoon honey, agave nectar, or maple syrup (optional)

JUST THE TIPS

Always use the freshest raw nuts to get the most flavor for your milk.

Avoid nuts with their skins on for a less chalky texture and increased flavor in your finished product.

You cannot oversoak your nuts! Soak for as little as 12 hours or as many as 48 hours for a silkier, tastier product.

Don't throw away your strained nut pulp. Freeze it to add to smoothies, bake with your granola, or add to your oatmeal, or dry it out in the oven and use it as nut meal.

Kombitcha

10 cups cold filtered water

8 bags black tea, or 2 to 3 tablespoons loose-leaf black tea (or a mix of green and black tea)

1 cup sugar

1 (12-ounce) package SCOBY starter

1 tablespoon distilled white vinegar (optional)

PREP TIME: 15 MINUTES   **COOK TIME:** 10 TO 14 DAYS
TOTAL TIME: 14 DAYS   **YIELD:** 8 TO 10 DRINKS

Since I'm a stomach-issue sufferer who's about one accident away from permanently replacing underwear with Depends, I rely on kombucha for its scientifically touted digestive benefits (come through, fermentation). It also helps that the drink is fizzy and fun and can be tailored with spices, herbs, and fruit juices to create surprisingly complex flavor profiles. The process is a bit laborious, though, especially making the SCOBY, but so is doing your nails or filing your taxes. These tasks are simply nonnegotiable and always pay off in the long run. (At least the first one. I somehow owed money two years ago and am still bitter about it.)

1   Sterilize a 1-gallon glass jar with boiling water. Set aside to dry.

2   In a medium saucepan, bring 2 cups of the filtered water to a boil. Remove from the heat and add the tea bags. Let sit for 5 minutes. Remove the tea bags and stir in the sugar until it dissolves. Transfer the sweetened tea to the sterilized jar. Fill the jar with the remaining 8 cups filtered water, leaving 3 to 4 inches of space at the top of the jar.

3   Check the temperature of the tea: it should be between 68°F and 88°F, (the ideal temperature is 76°). If the tea is too hot, it can damage the SCOBY. Add the entire package of SCOBY starter and give the tea a stir.

4   It's now time to test the pH of the tea. Dip a pH test strip in the tea mixture and compare its color with the color chart: the pH should be 4.5 or below. If the pH is too high, add the vinegar, stir, and test again.

5   Cover the top of the jar with a cotton cloth or a coffee filter and secure it with a rubber band. Set the jar in a warm place out of direct sunlight—the top of a cupboard is a good option. Let the brew sit for 7 to 14 days; do not move it.

6   At day 7, begin tasting your brew by using an eyedropper to draw a sample from the side of the jar, trying not to disturb the SCOBY culture that has formed on top of the brew. The longer the tea ferments, the more sugar molecules are eaten up, resulting in a less sweet tea. The end result should be slightly tart. If it tastes too sweet, cover the jar and let the kombucha continue to ferment. Check every day until the kombucha reaches your desired taste. If it's too tart, simply sweeten it during bottling and try fermenting it for fewer days next time.

7   Once your desired taste is reached, test the pH again. The ideal pH for kombucha is between 2.5 and 3.5.

8   Now it's time to bottle. Using clean hands, remove the SCOBY culture from the brew and place in a sterilized glass jar with at least 1 cup of the kombucha brew. This is your starter for next batch of kombucha! Cover with a cotton cloth and secure with a rubber band. Store in a warm, dark spot for up to a month until ready to brew your next batch.

9   Transfer the rest of the kombucha to sterilized glass mason jars, leaving about 1/2 inch of space at the top. Seal the jars with their lids and leave them at room temperature, out of direct sunlight, for 1 to 3 days to begin their second fermentation, when they will become carbonated. The longer you ferment it, the more carbonated it will be.

10 Refrigerate to stop the fermentation and carbonation. Store in the refrigerator for up to 1 month.

LITERALLY CAN'T EVEN
Black tea is ideal for kombucha, but green tea also works.
Or try using a blend of black and green tea leaves.

JUST THE TIPS
Use only glass containers when making kombucha. No metal or plastic.

The type of sugar matters. You may be tempted to substitute other sugars for regular granulated sugar, but refrain! Granulated sugar is the best for feeding yeast and bacteria.

Plan ahead! Kombucha is a labor of love and requires two fermentation periods—the first for developing the perfect balance of tart and sweet and the second for developing bubbles.

While your kombucha is fermenting, taste it daily. If you let it sit too long, the yeast will die once it eats all the sugar, resulting in a vinegary-tasting product. If you don't let it ferment long enough, your product will be a very sweet tea.

If your SCOBY develops any type of mold, throw it out and start all over with a new one.

THE MORE YOU GLOW
Since kombucha is a tea that has been fermented, it's a good source of probiotics, which are great for gut health. It's also rich in antioxidants.

The Skinniest Margarita in the Room

PREP TIME: 2 MINUTES **TOTAL TIME:** 2 MINUTES **YIELD:** 1 DRINK

Lime wedge, to rim and garnish

Ground Himalayan salt, to rim

Ice cubes

2 ounces tequila blanco

1 ounce orange liqueur

1½ ounces freshly squeezed lime juice (from 2 small limes)

If you haven't licked your Himalayan salt lamp yet, you're lying. But this time we're taking that Himalayan salt in granular form and using it to line the rim of a skinny margarita. Sure, having the bartender drop triple sec may be code for "mess me up until I forget my own name," but tequila has become my drink of choice because a) it actually makes my hangovers less severe; b) it's seemingly healthier because it isn't derived from a carb such as potatoes or barley; and c) skinny margaritas. No matter your reasoning, I think we can all agree that salt, sweet, and alcohol is a perfect trifecta. At least for me . . . every day . . . at five p.m., when my patience wears as thin as Calista Flockhart in *The Birdcage*.

JUST THE TIPS

Use a quality tequila. For a skinny margarita, you are omitting the sour mix that contains a lot of sugar and hides a lot of the flavor of the tequila. Use a tequila that you'd be happy to drink on its own.

Are your limes too firm? Roll them under your hand on the counter to loosen the juices. Still too hard? Pop them in the microwave for a couple of seconds, but make sure not to let them go too long or they will burst!

Want to make a frozen skinny margarita? Freeze your citrus juice in ice trays and blitz it with the tequila, orange liqueur, and ice in a blender.

1 Run a lime wedge around the rim of your glass; set the lime wedge aside for garnish. Pour the salt onto a plate and dip the rim of the glass in the salt to coat. Fill the glass with ice and set aside.

2 In a cocktail shaker filled with ice, combine the tequila, orange liqueur, and lime juice. Shake until chilled. Strain into the prepared glass and garnish with the lime wedge. Enjoy.

Moscow Ass

PREP TIME: 2 MINUTES   **TOTAL TIME:** 2 MINUTES   **YIELD:** 1 DRINK

Crushed ice

2 ounces vodka

1/2 ounce freshly squeezed lime juice (from 1 lime)

4 ounces ginger beer

Lime wedge, for garnish

Mint sprig, for garnish

My obsession with ginger knows no bounds, though I once dated one who was a serious ass. Ginger root, or rhizome, rather, is my one true love, with its surplus of health properties and delectably spicy notes. I put it on everything and in everything, and if there's an opportunity to sip it from an adorably hammered copper mug with a candied garnish, then you better believe I'm already there cheersing the bartender and talking about the meaning of life. Or why Jessica Simpson's gestation period seems to be that of an elephant. Her pregnancies last for three years, no?

Fill a copper mug with crushed ice. Add the vodka and lime juice, top with the ginger beer, and stir. Garnish with the lime wedge and mint sprig. Enjoy.

JUST THE TIPS

The type of ice matters here. Make sure to crush it! You can do this by pulsing the ice in a food processor or by putting it in a zip-top bag and breaking it up with a meat mallet.

It's not necessary, but a Moscow Ass arguably tastes better out of a copper mug.

Hot Damn Sriracha Bloody Mary

PREP TIME: 5 MINUTES   **TOTAL TIME:** 5 MINUTES   **YIELD:** 1 DRINK

It's no secret that I love hot and spicy food, so in addition to the hundred-plus people I'd like to *dracarys* on a daily basis, I'd do it to my Bloody to ensure it has extra heat. But since I don't have any dragons to fly, it only makes sense to incorporate my favorite condiment of all time, sriracha, into what is arguably the best hair-of-the-dog drink you can sip at brunch. I also am not the hugest fan of tomatoes (am I the only one who thinks they taste like dishwater?), so you know this ish has got to be good if it's hitting my tongue and getting me out of bed during a hangover.

1   Fill a pint glass with ice and set aside.

2   In a cocktail shaker filled with ice, combine the vodka, tomato juice, lemon juice, lime juice, horseradish, Worcestershire sauce, sriracha sauce, celery salt, and cumin. Give it a few shakes and strain into the prepared glass. Garnish with caper berries, cocktail onions, the celery stalk, and the lime and lemon wedges. Serve.

Ice cubes

2 ounces vodka

5 ounces tomato juice

$^1/_2$ ounce freshly squeezed lemon juice (from 1 medium lemon)

$^1/_2$ ounce freshly squeezed lime juice (from 1 medium lime)

$^3/_4$ teaspoon freshly grated horseradish

$^1/_4$ teaspoon Worcestershire sauce

$^3/_4$ teaspoon sriracha sauce

Pinch of celery salt

Pinch of ground cumin

Caper berries, for garnish (optional)

Pickled cocktail onions, for garnish (optional)

Celery stalk, for garnish

Lime wedge, for garnish

Lemon wedge, for garnish

LITERALLY CAN'T EVEN

Switch up the base of your Bloody Mary by using Clamato—tomato juice that has clam broth added to it.

Make a big batch for a party and set up a garnish bar for your guests to make their own personalized Bloody Marys. Garnish options: pickles, bacon, olives, celery, baby carrots, lemons, limes, cherry tomatoes, pickled green beans, deviled eggs, shrimp, crab legs— anything you like!

Instagram-Friendly Aperol Spritz

PREP TIME: 2 MINUTES   **TOTAL TIME:** 2 MINUTES   **YIELD:** 1 DRINK

Here's one for all you "micro-influencers" out there. During a summer trip in Europe, the Aperol Spritz was our go-to drink even before we knew about apps such as Facetune to enhance* bold colors and details for Instagram (*completely alter reality to create false perceptions about people, places, and things). That orange, guuuuuurrrlllllllll, it really pops and will have anyone envying your alfresco dining situation. And with only three ingredients, it is perhaps the easiest and most effective way to pretend those 102-degree temperatures feel like nothing (when the reality is that the sweaty spaghetti straps on your boho chic tank top are melting into fettuccine).

Fill a large wineglass with ice. Pour in the prosecco and Aperol. Top with the club soda. Garnish with the orange slice. Enjoy!

Ice cubes
3 ounces prosecco
2 ounces Aperol
1 ounce club soda
Orange slice, for garnish

LITERALLY CAN'T EVEN
While there's no need to improve this nearly perfect drink, here are a couple of ways to put a spin on the Aperol Spritz:

- Add a splash of fresh grapefruit or lemon juice.
- Garnish with a few slices of cucumber.
- Add a splash of gin or vodka.

Can't wait until aperitivo hour to have your spritz? Try making a frozen Aperol Spritz! Put the Aperol and prosecco in a blender with 2 cups ice. Blend until smooth. Pour into a glass and top with club soda.

Beychella-Body Lemonade Turned Summer Shandy

PREP TIME: 10 MINUTES **COOK TIME:** 5 MINUTES
TOTAL TIME: 15 MINUTES **YIELD:** 8 TO 10 DRINKS

8 cups cold water

2 cups freshly squeezed lemon juice (8 to 10 lemons)

1 tablespoon powdered stevia

1 lemon, sliced, plus more for garnish

Ice, for serving

A healthy lemonade can be detoxifying, and the best way to mess all of that up is to put it in some beer and create a shandy. If you're "being good," here is a great lemonade recipe that I think even Beyoncé could get behind. And since it's an inarguable fact that we should all aspire to be Queen Bey, that's all the justification I need. But yes, the diet-ruining beer part. We basics are typically fine with any light variety that's easy on calories but heavy on "I'm a fun girl!" vibes. And exes say we're difficult to please? Tell 'em, "Boy, bye."

In a large pitcher, combine the cold water, lemon juice, stevia, and lemon slices. Mix to combine. Transfer to the refrigerator to chill until ready to serve. Serve over ice, garnished with a lemon slice.

JUST THE TIPS

Making your own lemonade allows you to control the amount of sugar going into your drink.

Want to make sure your lemonade doesn't get watered down? Double the recipe and freeze half in ice cube trays. When you're ready to serve, use the frozen lemonade cubes instead of ice.

LITERALLY CAN'T EVEN

If you need a little something more with your lemonade that's equally refreshing, try making a shandy! Use equal parts your favorite light beer and lemonade, and garnish with a slice of lemon.

Craving something spicy? Add a splash of fresh ginger juice.

You Go, Glenn Hot Cocoa

PREP TIME: 5 MINUTES   **TOTAL TIME:** 5 MINUTES   **YIELD:** 1 DRINK

There's nothing I loathe more in life than the months of January to March. What is there to look forward to beyond layering your Burberry scarves for cold weather? Layering, in general, is probably the most annoying action in the entire world, only behind waiting in line at the DMV. Can you imagine having to layer up to wait in line at the DMV? Just throw me into oncoming traffic, please. My idea of winter perfection, however, is lying naked on a bearskin rug in a cabin by the fire, with jazz playing in the background, sipping a hot cocoa with literally no effs to give. And if I'm lucky enough to ever find myself in this setting (the Wall Street husband needs to swipe right on Tinder) and not in the slushy streets of New York, this is the cocoa I'd prefer to be consuming in mass quantities.

In a small saucepan over medium heat, combine the milk, coconut sugar, and cocoa powder, whisking to remove any lumps. When the milk is just at a low simmer, add the chocolate and stir until the chocolate melts. Stir in the vanilla, cayenne, cinnamon, and salt and remove from the heat. Pour into a large mug. Garnish with whipped cream, chocolate shavings, and additional cinnamon, along with the cinnamon stick and toasted marshmallows, if desired. Serve immediately.

1 cup whole milk

1 tablespoon coconut sugar

1 tablespoon unsweetened Dutch-process cocoa powder

2 ounces bittersweet chocolate, chopped

$1/4$ teaspoon vanilla extract

Pinch of cayenne pepper

Pinch of ground cinnamon, plus more for garnish

Pinch of kosher salt

Whipped cream, for garnish

Chocolate shavings, for garnish

Cinnamon stick, for garnish (optional)

Toasted marshmallows, for garnish (optional)

JUST THE TIPS

Your hot chocolate is only as good as the quality of the ingredients you put into it:

- Use Dutch-process cocoa powder.

- Use high-quality chocolate.

- Use whole milk (or, if you are dairy-free, nut/oat milk).

1 (750-milliliter) bottle
   prosecco or cava, chilled

1 cup pulp-free orange juice,
   chilled

JUST THE TIPS
Always serve your mimosas
in a champagne flute, with
or without a stem. There's
a reason champagne has its
own special glass: it helps
preserve the bubbles.

The Ultimate Mimosa Bar

PREP TIME: 2 MINUTES   **TOTAL TIME:** 2 MINUTES   **YIELD:** 6 TO 8 DRINKS

I know I'm not the only one who makes eye contact with a hot guy on the train and immediately thinks he's meant to be my boyfriend. After a mimosa-fueled brunch, he's meant to be my husband. And what's better than a mimosa? Well, a husband, I guess, but also a mimosa bar. I highly suggest buying more bubbly than you think you'll need, because you know your drunk-ass friends are going to pour as though they have Jaime Lannister's gold hand from *Game of Thrones*. Ultimately this is a cheers to bubbles, because a little fizz just gets us more excited than a sticker sale at Michaels.

Fill 6 to 8 champagne flutes halfway with prosecco. Top off with the orange juice. Serve.

LITERALLY CAN'T EVEN

Mimosas are classically made with orange juice, but feel free to put out an array of fruit juices to mix and match: grapefruit, mango, pineapple, pomegranate, cranberry, peach, pear, or any others. Just make sure they're 100 percent fruit juice.

The classic ratio is two parts champagne to one part juice, but feel free to adjust the ratio to whatever suits your taste buds.

Don't forget a fresh fruit garnish! Pomegranate seeds, fresh cranberries, pineapple, mango, slices of orange or grapefruit, anything you like.

Looking to make your mimosa extra special? Mix in a splash of elderflower or orange liqueur.

The Joejito

PREP TIME: 10 MINUTES   **TOTAL TIME:** 10 MINUTES PLUS COOLING
YIELD: 1 DRINK

My dad's cooking reminds me of businessmen in Hugo Boss suits wearing sneakers. But every once in a while he swaps the Keds for a pair of suede Ferragamos and gets it right. Those Ferragamos are his mojito . . . and it is perfection. I was upper middle class enough to have a lime tree in my backyard growing up in Florida, and my dad picked and juiced its limes consistently. The only problem is that he eyeballs everything he makes, and to get him to create an actual recipe was beyond pulling teeth. It was like pulling rotted gums, the tongue, and that dangling flap of skin in the back of your throat that surely has a scientific name I'll never remember. But alas, he caved, and this is the recipe I may or may not have blacked out on during multiple family gatherings.

1   First make the citrus-mint simple syrup: In a medium saucepan, combine the water and sugar and bring to a boil over high heat. Reduce the heat to maintain a simmer and stir until the sugar has dissolved. Remove from the heat and add the lime rind and mint sprigs. Let cool to room temperature. Transfer to an airtight container and refrigerate until ready to use, up to one month.

2   Slap 6 leaves from the mint sprigs into the palm of your hand to release their flavors. Put them at the bottom of a highball glass. Fill with ice and set aside.

3   In a shaker filled with ice, combine ¼ cup of the citrus-mint simple syrup, the lime rinds, lime juice, lemon juice, and white rum. Shake until chilled. Pour into the prepared glass and garnish with lemon and lime wedges and a mint sprig. Serve.

LITERALLY CAN'T EVEN
White rum is traditional, but feel free to
experiment with gold or dark.

FOR THE CITRUS-MINT SIMPLE SYRUP
½ cup water
½ cup sugar
1 lime rind
2 mint sprigs

2 mint sprigs
Ice cubes
3 ounces freshly squeezed lime juice, 4 rinds reserved
1 ounce freshly squeezed lemon juice (from 1 medium lemon)
2 ounces white rum
Lemon and lime wedges, for garnish

JUST THE TIPS
Never tear the leaves of your mint sprigs for your mojito; this allows the bitterness from the mint to enter the drink.

Don't overmuddle your mint leaves; instead, "slap" them in the palm of your hand to release their flavor.

Use a 1-1-2 ratio (lime–simple syrup–rum).

Snappy Apps

If Tyra Banks has two appetizers in her hands, store-bought vs. homemade, you better believe that the homemade option is staying and the store-bought must immediately pack its bags and go home.

But don't fret! Homemade doesn't have to require the finesse and attention of a gourmet chef. There are quick-and-easy basic bitch classics that you can prepare in literally 20 minutes or less. And do your guests have to know? Absolutely not. Part of a basic bitch's charm is her ability to mask a world of struggles with a smile and some avocado. So throw that picnic in the park and bask in the glory of being a better cook than your friends. Seeing the jealous frown on Becky's face as she sports her last-season Michael Kors watch and ponders why she isn't as cool as you is worth all the time and effort alone.

(2)

Simply Glorious Avocado Toast

PREP TIME: 15 MINUTES   **COOK TIME:** 10 MINUTES
TOTAL TIME: 25 MINUTES PLUS CHILLING   **YIELD:** 1 SERVING

I have a random obsession with gospel music, even though I'm pretty sure I'd burst into flames walking into any place of worship. But when I think of the basic bitch lifestyle, I hear large-framed, sequin-clad angels joining together in glorious sidestep to sing avocado toast's praises to the Lord Jesus. Can I get an *amen* on whole-grain toast topped with red pepper flakes and pickled red onions? *AMEN!* This recipe will turn you into a believer. And if not, it will at least keep you satiated on a Sunday morning when you have very few ingredients in your pantry, are recounting the previous night's sins, and need something to feel light as an angel (and that isn't a communion wafer).

1   First make the pickled red onions: Put the red onion in a large glass bowl. Set aside.

2   In a medium stockpot, combine the vinegar, sugar, salt, water, bay leaf, coriander, mustard seeds, peppercorns, and garlic. Bring to a boil and stir until the sugar and salt dissolve. Remove from the heat and pour over the red onion. Let sit until the liquid cools to room temperature. Transfer to an airtight container and refrigerate for at least 2 hours.

3   Mash the avocado slices onto the toast. Drizzle with the lemon juice and season with salt. Top with pickled red onion, micro cilantro, flaky sea salt, and red pepper flakes. Serve.

LITERALLY CAN'T EVEN

There are a world of possibilities on how to make your avocado toast, so don't limit yourself! If you prefer a more guacamole vibe, mash your avocado in a separate bowl with the addition of some lemon juice and salt before spreading it onto your toast. If mashed avocado isn't your thing, feel free to thinly slice and fan out the avocado. It not only looks pretty but tastes great!

Looking to add more protein to your avocado toast? Add some chickpeas or hummus with your avocado or top it with a fried egg.

FOR THE PICKLED RED ONIONS

1 red onion, peeled and thinly sliced

1 1/2 cups distilled white vinegar

1/4 cup sugar

2 teaspoons kosher salt

1 cup water

1 bay leaf

1 teaspoon coriander seeds

1/2 teaspoon mustard seeds

1/2 teaspoon black peppercorns

2 garlic cloves, thinly sliced

1/2 ripe avocado, thinly sliced

1 slice whole-grain bread, toasted

1 teaspoon freshly squeezed lemon juice

Kosher salt

Micro cilantro, for garnish

Flaky sea salt, for garnish

Red pepper flakes, for garnish

JUST THE TIPS

You'll want to use a perfectly ripe avocado for your toast. If there are any brown spots, cut them out.

Salt and acid are key when making avocado toast. Whether you are mashing the avocado or slicing it, make sure that you are seasoning as you go.

Spinach and Artichoke's High School Reunion Dip

PREP TIME: 15 MINUTES **COOK TIME:** 15 MINUTES
TOTAL TIME: 30 MINUTES **YIELD:** 10 TO 12 SERVINGS (4 CUPS)

Oh, the days of high school, when I would order this and assume I was checking off my veggie servings on the food pyramid. Now I don't have to worry about a food pyramid or what shape my body resembles because I eat this in bed, with Hulu, and judge anyone who believes their Friday night plans at a dive bar or apartment party are better than mine. Because *they're not!* The beauty of this dip is that you can use fresh or canned varieties of either vegetable, though you should certainly aim for the former, because every self-help book keeps telling you to "love yourself." Wow! Riveting! Never heard that one before.

1 pumpernickel boule

2 tablespoons olive oil

2 tablespoons unsalted butter

1 shallot, minced

2 large garlic cloves, minced

1 pound fresh spinach, finely chopped, or 1 (10-ounce) package frozen spinach, defrosted, drained, and chopped

Kosher salt and freshly ground black pepper

Pinch of red pepper flakes

1 (12-ounce) jar quartered artichoke hearts, drained and chopped

1 cup packed grated fresh mozzarella cheese

6 ounces cream cheese, cut into 1-inch cubes

1/2 cup sour cream or plain full-fat Greek yogurt

1/2 cup mayonnaise

1/2 cup freshly grated Parmesan cheese

1 Leaving a 2-inch border, cut the center out of the pumpernickel boule, creating a bowl for your dip. Cut the bread from the center into bite-size pieces. Set aside until ready to serve.

2 In a straight-sided large skillet, heat the olive oil and butter over medium-high heat. Add the shallot and sauté until translucent, about 3 minutes. Add the garlic and cook until fragrant, about 30 seconds. Add the spinach a handful at a time, stirring to wilt. Season with salt and black pepper and a pinch of red pepper flakes. Cook until all the excess liquid from the spinach has evaporated, about 4 minutes. Add the artichokes and cook until heated through, about 2 minutes.

3 Reduce the heat to medium-low and add the mozzarella and cream cheese. Stir until the cheeses have melted. Add the sour cream, mayonnaise, and Parmesan. Taste and adjust the seasoning. Transfer to your prepared bread bowl and serve with the bread cubes for dipping.

JUST THE TIPS

You can serve this spinach-and-artichoke dip with chips, a bread bowl, crackers, or vegetable crudités, but make sure it remains warm by keeping it in a slow cooker or on the stove.

If you're pressed for time, feel free to use frozen spinach. Just make sure to defrost the spinach and wring out all the excess liquid.

All Hail the Kale (and Other Veggie) Chips

PREP TIME: 20 MINUTES   **COOK TIME:** 25 MINUTES
TOTAL TIME: 45 MINUTES   **YIELD:** 4 SERVINGS

1 bunch kale, washed and dried
2 tablespoons olive oil
Za'atar (optional)
Kosher salt

Kale chips can seriously go eff themselves. I want to hate them, I really do, but they're just so damn addictive and such a perfect substitute for actual chips that I can house them by the bag in one sitting. Now listen, I'm not going to sit here and pretend that these are better than any potato variety. People who mutter such atrocities can't be trusted . . . ever . . . even in a game of Monopoly. But what I will tell you is that these and other veggie chips are perfect vessels for salt and seasonings, to distract you from the fact that they're healthy. And when it comes to the mundanity of everyday life, I'll take distractions in any form.

1   Preheat the oven to 275°F.

2   Stem the kale and tear the leaves into bite-size pieces. Toss the kale with the olive oil to coat, massaging the oil into the leaves gently. Sprinkle with za'atar, if using, and season with salt. Spread evenly in a single layer on two baking sheets and transfer to the oven. Bake until crispy, rotating the pans halfway through, 25 to 30 minutes. Remove from the oven and serve.

LITERALLY CAN'T EVEN
Looking to make other vegetable chips, such as beet or sweet potato chips? Using a mandoline, slice the vegetables very thin. Toss with olive oil, season with salt, and bake in a preheated 375°F oven for 15 to 20 minutes, until crisp. Remove from the oven and let cool before serving.

BASIC BASICS

While you could buy already chopped kale in a bag, you run the risk of the large, woody stems being included. I prefer to buy a bunch of kale and stem it myself, then breaking up the leaves into bite-size pieces by hand.

Wash and dry your kale completely before roasting. Excess moisture on the kale will result is a less crispy chip.

Massage the oil into your kale. Kale is a sturdy green and can benefit from a quick oil massage to soften it.

Make sure your chips are spread out in an even layer on your baking sheet, not overlapping, for best results.

Dangerously Delicious Pita Chips and Millennial Pink Hummus

PREP TIME: 15 MINUTES **COOK TIME:** 30 MINUTES
TOTAL TIME: 45 MINUTES **YIELD:** 8 TO 10 SERVINGS

There have been a few times when I've essentially needed stitches for cutting my lip on a pita chip. When I'm noshing on snacks, I go hard, and since I eat hummus every day of my life (#fact), the possibility of injury increases drastically. This probability is at an all-time high when I pair the hazardous chip with a beautiful pink beet hummus. And not just any pink . . . millennial pink, the rosé-hued, subdued version of Barbie's signature Corvette that has graced pedicures, Rent the Runway gowns, and Jeffree Star YouTube videos for years. Now if only our older generation can give us a stable economy and competent politicians, we'll give you more millennial-inspired foods.

1 First make the pita chips: Preheat the oven to 375°F. In a large bowl, toss the pita wedges with the olive oil and season with salt. Divide the pita wedges evenly between two baking sheets in a single layer. Bake until crisp, 10 to 12 minutes, rotating the trays halfway through. Remove from the oven and let cool. Raise the oven temperature to 400°F.

2 Make the toasted chickpeas: In a large bowl, combine the chickpeas, olive oil, and salt and toss to coat evenly. Add to a baking sheet in a single layer. Roast, stirring occasionally, for 35 to 40 minutes, until crispy on the outside. Remove from the oven and toss to coat with the cumin, coriander, and sumac. Set aside.

3 Meanwhile, make the hummus: In a medium saucepot, combine the chickpeas, baking soda, 1 garlic clove, the bay leaf, and water to cover and bring to a boil over high heat. Reduce the heat to medium and boil for 15 to 20 minutes, until the chickpeas begin to break down and their skins loosen. Drain the chickpeas, discarding the garlic and bay leaf.

4 In a blender, combine the lemon juice, remaining garlic clove, beet, and a generous pinch each of salt and pepper. Blend until the garlic and beet are finely chopped. Add the tahini and cumin and blend to combine. Add the chickpeas and blend until smooth. If the mixture becomes too thick, add a few tablespoons of water. With the blender running on low, drizzle in the olive oil. Taste and adjust the seasoning. Transfer to a serving bowl and chill until ready to serve. Garnish with the toasted chickpeas, a drizzle of olive oil, and chopped parsley. Serve with the pita chips.

FOR THE PITA CHIPS
8 pitas, separated and cut into 8 wedges each
¹/₄ cup olive oil
Kosher salt

FOR THE TOASTED CHICKPEAS
1 (15-ounce) can chickpeas, drained, rinsed, and dried
2 tablespoons olive oil
¹/₂ teaspoon kosher salt
¹/₄ teaspoon ground cumin
¹/₄ teaspoon ground coriander
¹/₄ teaspoon ground sumac

FOR THE HUMMUS
1 (15-ounce) can chickpeas, drained and rinsed
³/₄ teaspoon baking soda
2 large garlic cloves
1 bay leaf
¹/₃ cup freshly squeezed lemon juice (from 2 to 3 lemons)
1 small red beet, roasted, peeled, and diced
Kosher salt and freshly ground black pepper
¹/₂ cup tahini
³/₄ teaspoon ground cumin
2 tablespoons olive oil, plus more for serving
Chopped fresh flat-leaf parsley, for garnish

JUST THE TIPS

For the creamiest hummus, make sure you use overcooked chickpeas. You can absolutely start with dried chickpeas and make this from scratch, but canned chickpeas work just fine.

Add a bit of baking soda to raise the pH of the water you boil your chickpeas in. This will help the chickpeas break down, resulting in the perfect product for a creamy hummus.

"I'm Like, 75 Percent Italian" Bruschetta

PREP TIME: 20 MINUTES   **COOK TIME:** 5 MINUTES
TOTAL TIME: 25 MINUTES   **YIELD:** 8 SERVINGS

I'm that annoying person who was once corrected by an equally annoying person on how to properly pronounce "bruschetta." The "ch" sound is more like a "k." K? And despite the fact that my great-grandmother Vincenza Albanese is probably rolling in her grave over my frequent attempts to speak proper Italian, I wear my heritage like a badge of honor, sans the tragic graphic T-shirts and excess hair spray associated with self-proclaimed guidos. But what makes up for my inability to speak the native tongue? This garlicky bruschetta, of course. Just one bite will have you assuming that I sip *caffès*, wear head-to-toe Gucci, and hang a poster of Sophia Loren eating rigatoni in my bedroom. *Mangia!*

FOR THE TOMATOES

- 1 pound heirloom cherry tomatoes, cut into ¹/₂-inch dice
- 2 tablespoons minced shallot
- 1 garlic clove, minced (optional)
- 1 tablespoon sherry vinegar
- 1 tablespoon olive oil
- Kosher salt and freshly ground black pepper

FOR THE WHIPPED RICOTTA

- ³/₄ cup fresh whole-milk ricotta
- 2 tablespoons olive oil
- ¹/₂ teaspoon kosher salt
- ¹/₄ teaspoon freshly ground black pepper

- 1 baguette, sliced on the bias ¹/₂ inch thick
- 3 tablespoons olive oil
- Kosher salt
- 2 garlic cloves
- ¹/₄ cup julienned fresh basil leaves
- Olive oil, for drizzling
- Flaky sea salt, for garnish

1. First make the tomatoes: Preheat the broiler. In a large bowl, combine the tomatoes, shallot, garlic (if using), vinegar, and olive oil. Season with salt and pepper. Set aside for at least 10 minutes and up to 1 hour.

2. Meanwhile, make the whipped ricotta: In a food processor, combine the ricotta, olive oil, salt, and pepper. Process until smooth, 1 to 2 minutes. Taste and adjust the seasonings. Set aside.

3. Spread the baguette slices in an even layer across two baking sheets. Drizzle both sides with olive oil and season with salt. Transfer to the oven to toast for about 1 minute per side. Remove from the oven and rub the garlic cloves over the slices of bread. Let cool.

4. Spread a thin layer of whipped ricotta over the toasted baguette slices and top with the tomato mixture. Garnish with the basil, a drizzle of olive oil, and a little flaky sea salt. Serve immediately.

LITERALLY CAN'T EVEN

Mix up your tomato varieties. Use different heirloom tomatoes along with cherry tomatoes for a blend of flavors.

JUST THE TIPS

Bruschetta is a simple dish that has one main rule to follow: Use only the freshest ingredients. Tomatoes are in season in the summer, and you want to use only those tomatoes that are picked at the peak of ripeness.

Garlic is an essential component of this bruschetta. Rub a peeled clove over the freshly toasted slices of bread to extract the flavor. This is what Italians call a *fettunta*.

Five-Star Guacamole

PREP TIME: 15 MINUTES   **TOTAL TIME:** 15 MINUTES
YIELD: 10 TO 12 SERVINGS (3 CUPS)

4 ripe avocados, peeled and pitted

3 tablespoons freshly squeezed lemon juice (from about 2 lemons)

$^1/_2$ teaspoon ground cumin

Kosher salt

1 small jalapeño, seeds and ribs removed, finely diced

$^1/_4$ cup finely diced red onion

1 Roma tomato, seeded and small diced

$^1/_4$ cup fresh cilantro leaves, finely chopped

JUST THE TIPS

Wondering how to pick the perfect avocado? Gently squeeze the avocado in your hand; a perfect avocado will be firm but yield to some pressure. Unripe avocados will remain hard.

Need to ripen your avocados? Place them in a brown paper bag, add an apple, and close the bag. Apples naturally release ethylene, which speeds up the ripening process by 2 to 3 days.

I'm going to make enemies by saying this, but I never really crave Mexican food (or at least Americanized versions of it). It's fine, I'll devour a taco or seven when they're in front of me, but it's not my go-to cuisine like Asian, Italian, or deep-fried American. Guacamole, on the other hand, is something I crave on a daily basis and pretty much make on the weekly. When it comes to apps, I give it five stars, like the Uber driver who recently sang Ariana Grande's "No Tears Left to Cry" with me in not-so-perfect harmony (it's the thought that counts). This variation, which really highlights the fresh cilantro, also deserves five stars. So swipe right, *chica*, and start pickin' it up, pickin' it up . . . with a tortilla chip, of course.

1   In a large bowl, mash together the avocados, lemon juice, cumin, and salt to taste, making sure to leave the mixture a little chunky. Fold in the jalapeño, red onion, tomato, and cilantro. Taste and adjust the seasoning.

2   Serve immediately, or cover the bowl with plastic wrap pressed directly against the surface of the guacamole to prevent browning and refrigerate for up to 2 days.

Soul Mate Queso Dip

PREP TIME: 10 MINUTES **COOK TIME:** 15 MINUTES
TOTAL TIME: 25 MINUTES **YIELD:** 12 SERVINGS (4 CUPS)

I'd like to shake the hand of the person who decided to melt cheese, add jalapeño, and dip things into it. That person is my kind of person, and I think we would have been super compatible. If you're a keto queen, you can also substitute vegetables for the chips and go carb-free crazy. If you're a carb queen, like me, you can figure out other types of carbs to dip into the cheesy goodness. The possibilities are endless, unlike the lie of "the possibilities are endless" that your parents and teachers preached during your adolescence. I'd like my money back, please. And by money, I mean childhood life lessons.

1   Heat the olive oil in a medium pot over medium-high heat. Add the onion, bell pepper, garlic, jalapeños, and a generous pinch of salt and cook, stirring, until very soft, about 7 minutes.

2   Reduce the heat to medium-low, add the cream, and bring to a simmer. Add the cheeses and cook, stirring continuously, until melted. Add the green chilies, taste, and adjust the seasoning. Serve warm, garnished with cilantro, if desired, with the tortilla chips on the side.

1 tablespoon olive oil

1 small white onion, peeled and finely diced (about 1 cup)

1 red bell pepper, seeded and finely diced (about 1 cup)

2 cloves garlic, minced

2 to 3 jalapeños, seeds removed if not a fan of heat, finely diced, (about 1/3 cup)

Kosher salt

1 1/4 cups heavy cream

12 ounces yellow American cheese, grated (3 cups)

6 ounces pepper Jack cheese, grated (1 1/2 cups)

1 (4-ounce) can diced green chilies

1/4 cup chopped fresh cilantro, for garnish (optional)

Tortilla chips, for serving

JUST THE TIPS

For a melty queso, make sure to *always* buy full blocks of cheese and grate them yourself at home. It may take a little more effort, but pre-shredded cheese is coated in anticlumping agents that prevent you from getting the ooey-gooey queso you've been looking for.

Looking for a block of American cheese? Go to the deli counter of your local grocery store and ask for one.

Nacho Average Nachos

PREP TIME: 15 MINUTES **COOK TIME:** 10 MINUTES
TOTAL TIME: 25 MINUTES **YIELD:** 10 TO 12 SERVINGS

My favorite pastime is creating dishes in the form of literal mountains and challenging myself to see if I can rappel down them to the plate. This makes me the textbook definition of skinny-fat, but I could be addicted to meth instead, so fight me. Perhaps the most fun mountain to make is one of nachos, loaded with ingredient after ingredient so that no two bites are exactly the same. It's not difficult to make and, once I swap my summer bod for my dad bod in the winter, serves as a perfect substitute for a warm boyfriend. Who needs human touch? Not this guy. (Unless that human is bringing nachos.)

1 In a large nonstick skillet over medium heat, cook the chorizo, breaking it up with a potato masher, until well browned and cooked through, about 5 minutes. Add the onion and beans and cook until the onion softens and the beans warm through, about 4 minutes. Drain on a paper towel–lined plate.

2 Scatter the blue and yellow tortilla chips over a serving platter. Top evenly with the queso dip, chorizo mixture, pico de gallo, guacamole, crema, jalapeño, cotija, scallions, and cilantro. Serve immediately.

$^1/_2$ pound fresh (Mexican) chorizo, casings removed

$^1/_2$ small white onion, finely chopped

1 (15-ounce) can pinto beans, drained and rinsed

$^1/_2$ (8-ounce) bag blue corn tortilla chips

$^1/_2$ (8-ounce) bag yellow corn tortilla chips

1 cup Soul Mate Queso Dip (page 55)

$^1/_2$ cup pico de gallo

$^1/_3$ cup Five-Star Guacamole (page 54)

$^1/_4$ cup crema

$^1/_4$ cup sliced pickled jalapeño (optional)

$^1/_4$ cup crumbled cotija cheese

2 small scallions, thinly sliced on the bias ($^1/_4$ cup)

$^1/_4$ cup fresh cilantro leaves

JUST THE TIPS

There is a balance to the art of nacho-making. No one likes a soggy nacho, but equally as bad is the bottom of the nacho plate having just chips with no topping. Tips for getting the perfect plate of nachos:

- Make sure to choose a sturdy chip that can handle the weight of the toppings.

- Layer the nachos so that you have toppings on each chip for the perfect bite. One layer of nachos is great. Two layers of nachos is even better.

- You have two paths to pick from with nachos: either you can make a fresh queso sauce or you can shred cheese to melt on your nachos. Either is delicious. Or even better, opt for both!

3 tablespoons unsalted butter

1 tablespoon olive oil

¹/₂ teaspoon garlic powder

¹/₂ teaspoon onion powder

¹/₄ teaspoon dried oregano

¹/₄ teaspoon dried basil

¹/₄ teaspoon dried thyme

Pinch of kosher salt

**1 small baguette, cut into
¹/₂-inch cubes (about 4 cups)**

FOR THE SALAD

1 garlic clove, cut into quarters

¹/₃ cup olive oil

**¹/₂ teaspoon kosher salt, plus
more for seasoning**

**¹/₈ teaspoon freshly ground
black pepper, plus more for
seasoning**

**1¹/₂ to 2 romaine hearts,
torn into bite-size pieces
(about 8 cups)**

1 egg

**2 tablespoons freshly squeezed
lemon juice (from 1 medium
lemon)**

1 cup seasoned croutons

**¹/₄ cup freshly grated Parmesan
cheese**

6 anchovy fillets (optional)

JUST THE TIPS

Traditionally, Caesar salad was made tableside by a waiter dressed in a tuxedo who could toss together romaine lettuce, a whole egg, cheese, and garlic. Yes, a whole egg.

While most dressing can be made in advance, this dressing, because of the raw egg, should be made the day you are planning to use it. While it's safe for healthy adults to consume raw eggs, those with compromised immune systems, the elderly, and pregnant women should avoid them.

Mom's Definitely-Not-Sicilian Sicilian Caesar Salad

PREP TIME: 10 MINUTES   **COOK TIME:** 30 MINUTES
TOTAL TIME: 40 MINUTES   **YIELD:** 4 TO 6 SERVINGS

I didn't grow up on a creamy Caesar. Instead, it was my mom's garlicky version that she would credit to her rustic roots and Sicilian heritage. But after doing some research (read: Google), I found that Caesar's roots are not only *not* in Italy, they're totally Sun-In! (I knew he wasn't a natural blond.) My other, perhaps more relevant discovery was that there seems to be no trace of a "Sicilian Caesar" in existence. So this is a Caesar that is actually sans predictable mayonnaise, and with an egg, lemon juice, and lots of garlic instead: a Caesar that has spent a few too many hours on the beaches of Tulum, has basted in bronzer, and is dying to let you know that it visited its grandmother in Italy once and has the Instagrams to prove it. Either way, it's delicious and perfect for a dinner party with guests who have last names that end in vowels. And if you want to make it authentically Robin (my mom), be sure to serve it with lots of love, but also a backhanded compliment that leads to dramatic hand movements and unnecessary F-bombs. Ah, the tastes of home.

1   First make the seasoned croutons: Preheat the oven to 350°F. In a small saucepan over medium heat, combine the butter, olive oil, garlic powder, onion powder, oregano, basil, thyme, and salt. Cook until the butter is melted and the flavors are combined, 2 to 3 minutes. Remove from the heat. (If not using immediately, store in an airtight container at room temperature for up to 3 days or in the freezer for up to 1 month.)

2   Put the bread cubes in a large bowl and pour the butter mixture over them. Toss to coat, then spread the cubes on a baking sheet in a single even layer. Transfer to the oven and bake for 12 to 15 minutes, tossing halfway through, until light brown and toasted. Remove from the oven and let cool.

3   Make the salad: In a small bowl, marinate the garlic in olive oil for 30 minutes. Stir in the salt and pepper. Place the romaine lettuce in a large salad bowl. Remove the garlic pieces from the oil, discard the garlic, and pour the oil over the romaine. Toss lightly. Season with salt and pepper. Break the egg over the salad, add the lemon juice, and toss again. Add the croutons and Parmesan. Garnish with the anchovies, if using. Serve immediately.

Nuts About Nut Butter

4 cups raw nuts (almonds, walnuts, peanuts, hazelnuts, any kind you prefer)

³/₄ teaspoon sea salt

JUST THE TIPS

This may come as a shock, but a true nut butter has just one ingredient: nuts! While I like to add a little salt, you don't need to add anything to develop a creamy texture. Just have the patience to wait the 25 minutes for the nuts to break down.

PREP TIME: 5 MINUTES **COOK TIME:** 30 MINUTES
TOTAL TIME: 35 MINUTES **YIELD:** 2 CUPS

Choosy moms may choose Jif, but smart moms choose to make their own nut butter. It's free of added oils, sugars, and preservatives and can include your favorite nut or seed. Macadamia is my personal favorite, although anything fattening or Hawaiian is finding its way into my mouth lately. I blame Moana, who seems to have more of an influence on my life than Alanis Morissette did in the 1990s. Isn't it ironic? Don't you think? No. It's not. Much like everything in the song, which actually makes it ironic. We don't deserve you, Alanis. Nor do we deserve this super-easy-to-make recipe that you can easily spread on what is, perhaps, the most basic grocery item of all: rice cakes.

1 Preheat the oven to 350°F.

2 Spread the nuts over a baking sheet and toast in the oven for about 5 minutes, until fragrant. Remove from the oven and transfer to a food processor or blender. Add the salt. Process the nuts until they transform into a creamy butter, scraping down the sides of the bowl or blender jar as needed, about 25 minutes. Once the nut butter is creamy, store it in an airtight container in the refrigerator for up to 1 month.

LITERALLY CAN'T EVEN
Have fun here and try out different add-ins to create your own blend of nut butter. Think maple syrup, vanilla extract, chia seeds, flaxseed, cinnamon, or even chocolate!

Don't forget about seed butter. Sunflower seeds are a delicious option.

Dentist-Hating (or -Loving?) Popcorn

PREP TIME: 5 MINUTES **COOK TIME:** 5 MINUTES
TOTAL TIME: 10 MINUTES **YIELD:** 7 CUPS POPCORN

I need someone to invent a contraption that slices my hand off when I reach for snacks. And since popcorn is the one snack with which I surrender all self-control, this contraption would be an ideal gift, like . . . yesterday. Popcorn's versatility is what makes it a star. You can coat it with literally anything, making it sweet, salty, healthy, and even bougie (hi, truffle salt and saffron). The only problem is that I smash popcorn into my mouth by the fistful, leading to kernel shells spot-welded to the roof of my mouth for days . . . weeks, even. This reinforces the fact that I may be one of the world's most disgusting humans, but I'll take any excuse to visit my hot dentist and open wide.

1 Using an air popper, pop the popcorn kernels into a large serving bowl.

2 For the coconut oil–nutritional yeast variety: Drizzle the coconut oil over the popped popcorn. Sprinkle with the nutritional yeast and season with salt.

For the ranch variety: Drizzle the melted butter over the popped popcorn. Sprinkle with the ranch seasoning and chopped chives.

For the garlic, rosemary, and Parmesan variety: In a small saucepan, combine the olive oil, garlic, and rosemary. Heat for 1 minute, until the garlic is fragrant, then remove from the heat. Drizzle the olive oil mixture over the popped popcorn. Sprinkle with the Parmesan and season with salt.

3 Enjoy.

BASIC BASICS

If you don't have an air popper, you can either microwave popcorn kernels in a brown paper bag with the top rolled down to seal it or pop them in a pot on the stove. For the stovetop option, add a bit of oil to the pan and 1 kernel over medium heat. Wait for the kernel to pop, remove the piece of popcorn (chef snack!), and add the remaining kernels. Cover with a lid and cook until you stop hearing the kernels popping as frequently. Remove from the heat and wait a minute before removing the lid. You could also use a bag of lightly salted microwave popcorn that doesn't have any butter.

1/4 cup popcorn kernels

FOR THE COCONUT OIL–NUTRITIONAL YEAST VARIETY

3 tablespoons coconut oil, melted

1/4 cup nutritional yeast

Fine sea salt

FOR THE RANCH VARIETY

3 to 4 tablespoons unsalted butter, melted

2 tablespoons ranch seasoning mix

1 tablespoon chopped fresh chives

FOR THE GARLIC, ROSEMARY, AND PARMESAN VARIETY

3 tablespoons olive oil

2 garlic cloves, finely grated

2 teaspoons finely chopped fresh rosemary

1/4 cup freshly grated Parmesan cheese

Fine sea salt

THE MORE YOU GLOW

Nutritional yeast is grown to be used as a food product. Vegans typically use it as a replacement for the nutty, savory flavor of cheese. It's also a good source of B vitamins.

Bro-tastic Baked Chicken Wings

PREP TIME: 10 MINUTES   **COOK TIME:** 1 HOUR
TOTAL TIME: 1 HOUR 10 MINUTES   **YIELD:** 4 SERVINGS

2 teaspoons cornstarch

¼ cup water

4 garlic cloves, minced

1 (2-inch) piece fresh ginger, peeled and grated

3 tablespoons soy sauce

⅓ cup honey

¼ cup freshly squeezed lime juice (from about 2 limes)

2 teaspoons red pepper flakes (optional)

2 pounds chicken wings, separated and tips removed

2 tablespoons vegetable oil

Kosher salt and freshly ground black pepper

2 tablespoons sliced scallions, for garnish

1 tablespoon toasted white sesame seeds, for garnish

JUST THE TIPS

If you have the time, season your chicken wings and let them sit overnight in the fridge, uncovered. Remove them from the fridge and let them come to room temperature before baking.

I come from a huge football family, so you can imagine how thrilled my dad was when I asked for a Barbie after being potty trained and to be enrolled in gymnastics classes the year after that. In actuality, my dad is and has always been extremely supportive of me and my lack of football genetics, but one game-day commonality we share is a severe love for chicken wings. Seriously, I can morph into John Madden (with better clothes), talk pigskin, and root for the Steelers as long as there's some sort of wing involved. I'll even engage in stereotypically masculine activities, such as those god-awful bro-tastic handshakes or allowing my eyebrows to grow in—all for a delightfully spicy and crispy piece of chicken. But don't get me started on the ranch vs. blue cheese dressing debate. I side with the latter in this food version of *Sophie's Choice*.

1   Preheat the oven to 425°F. Line two rimmed baking sheets with foil.

2   In a small bowl, whisk together the cornstarch and water. Set aside. In a small saucepan over medium-high heat, combine the garlic, ginger, soy sauce, honey, lime juice, and red pepper flakes, if using. Heat until the honey dissolves. Whisk in the cornstarch mixture and heat until the glaze thickens, 2 to 3 minutes. Remove from the heat.

3   In a large bowl, toss the chicken wings with the vegetable oil and season with salt and black pepper. Divide the wings evenly between the two prepared baking sheets and bake for 40 minutes, rotating the pan halfway through, until crispy. Spread the glaze evenly over the wings and bake for an additional 5 to 7 minutes, until the glaze is bubbling and caramelized. Transfer to a serving platter, garnish with the scallions and sesame seeds, and serve.

LITERALLY CAN'T EVEN

If you prefer a Buffalo chicken wing, simply bake the wings as written, toss in ¼ cup Buffalo sauce and 4 tablespoons melted unsalted butter, and serve!

Diet-Ruining Mozzarella Sticks

PREP TIME: 25 MINUTES   **COOK TIME:** 1 HOUR 10 MINUTES
TOTAL TIME: 1 HOUR 35 MINUTES PLUS FREEZING   **YIELD:** 18 PIECES

Me every Sunday: "I want to start a diet, but I also want to coat cheese in bread crumbs and fry it." This weekly struggle has led to a perfect mozzarella stick recipe and a not-so-perfect duo of love handles. I volley between whether I prefer to be skinny or temporarily satiated, though cheese typically wins, and unsurprisingly so. Is there anyone in the world who can resist gooey, cheesy amazingness drenched in marinara sauce? If that anyone is you, then you need to reconsider your priorities. Denying yourself cheese is Stephanie Tanner levels of *rude*, and I'm simply not here for it.

1   Set a wire rack in a baking sheet and coat with nonstick spray.

2   Cut the mozzarella into ½ by 3-inch sticks (you should have about 18). Set up a dredging station using three shallow dishes. Put the flour in one and season with salt. Put the eggs and cream in the second dish and whisk to combine. In the final dish, combine the panko, garlic, onion, basil, parsley, and oregano and season with salt.

3   Dredge 1 piece of mozzarella in the flour, dip it in the egg mixture, and roll it in the panko mixture to coat all sides. Dip the mozzarella stick back in the egg mixture, followed by the panko. Transfer to the prepared rack. Repeat with the remaining mozzarella. Freeze the mozzarella sticks for at least 1 hour before frying.

4   In a large Dutch oven, heat the vegetable oil to 360°F. Remove the mozzarella sticks from the freezer and, working in batches of 4 or 5 at a time, fry the mozzarella sticks until golden brown, 2 to 3 minutes. Transfer back to the wire rack, season lightly with salt, and repeat with the remaining mozzarella sticks. Serve with the Pomodoro sauce.

(1-pound) block mozzarella cheese

¹/₂ cup all-purpose flour

Kosher salt

4 eggs

1 tablespoon heavy cream

2¹/₂ cups panko bread crumbs

1¹/₄ teaspoons minced garlic

1¹/₄ teaspoons minced onion

³/₄ teaspoon dried basil

³/₄ teaspoon dried parsley

¹/₂ teaspoon dried oregano

4 cups vegetable oil, for frying

Pomodoro sauce (page 121) or your favorite jarred sauce, for serving

JUST THE TIPS

For this recipe, stay away from fresh mozzarella. It will not hold up as well as the processed favorite, Polly-O.

Highway to Hell Soft Pretzels

PREP TIME: 10 MINUTES **COOK TIME:** 1 HOUR 30 MINUTES
TOTAL TIME: 1 HOUR 40 MINUTES **YIELD:** 8 PRETZELS

Every time I walk by an Auntie Anne's without buying something, a small part of my soul escapes through my nose and dies. When I realized there was very little of my soul left, I decided it'd be best to concoct my own soft pretzel recipe and secure a spot in, well, purgatory. (There are some things that I'm going to have to explain.) I'm convinced, though, that if given the opportunity to bake God some of these soft pretzels (with spicy mustard, of course), He'll certainly admit me to heaven. And if He doesn't, then I'll see the rest of you all in what I imagine to be a giant hot tub with lots of horns, pitchforks, and questionably fashionable Speedos emblazoned with flames.

1½ cups warm water
   (between 110° and 115°F)
1 tablespoon kosher salt
1 tablespoon sugar
1 (¼-ounce) packet active dry
   yeast (2¼ teaspoons)
2 tablespoons unsalted butter,
   melted
4 cups all-purpose flour,
   plus more for dusting
Vegetable oil, for brushing
½ cup baking soda
½ cup water
Coarse sea salt, for topping
Spicy mustard, for serving

1   In the bowl of a stand mixer, combine the warm water, salt, and sugar. Sprinkle the yeast on top and let sit until foaming, about 5 minutes. Add the melted butter and flour and, using the dough hook, mix on low speed. Once blended, increase speed to medium until the dough pulls from the sides and comes together and forms a ball. Transfer the dough to an oiled bowl and cover the bowl with plastic wrap. Place in a warm spot to proof for 1 hour, or until the dough has doubled in size.

2   Preheat the oven to 425°F. Line two baking sheets with parchment paper and brush the parchment with oil.

3   Turn the dough out onto a well-oiled work surface. Divide it into 8 equal pieces about 1½ inches thick and 8 inches long. Roll one piece into a 22-inch-long rope. Gather the ends of the rope and bring them together, creating a circle. Twist the ends and pull them forward, pressing them against the base of the circle to form a pretzel shape. Transfer to the prepared baking sheet and repeat with the remaining pieces of dough.

4   In a small bowl, mix the baking soda and water. Bring 7½ cups water to a boil in a large pot and add the baking soda mixture. Drop the pretzels into the water, one at a time, and boil for 30 seconds. Remove from the water with a slotted spoon and place back on the prepared baking sheet. Sprinkle with coarse sea salt. Repeat with the remaining pretzels.

5   Transfer the baking sheets to the oven and bake the pretzels until golden brown, 12 to 15 minutes. Remove from the oven and serve with mustard.

Insta-Worthy Farmers' Market Caprese Salad with Burrata

PREP TIME: 10 MINUTES **TOTAL TIME:** 10 MINUTES
YIELD: 6 TO 8 SERVINGS

4 to 6 heirloom tomatoes in a variety of colors, sliced and wedged

1 (7- to 8-ounce) ball or 2 (4-ounce) balls fresh burrata cheese

1 cup fresh basil leaves

¼ cup extra-virgin olive oil

3 tablespoons good-quality balsamic vinegar (such as Artigianale)

Flaky sea salt

Fresh coarsely ground black pepper

Be it colorful cakes, J.Crew sweaters, or three shades of drugstore foundation, basic bitches love to layer (I am the exception, as noted on page 39). It only makes sense to layer food, too, and caprese—when done meticulously—is layering at its finest. But I have to preface this recipe by declaring that the best caprese salads come only from a trip to the farmers' market. So if you're not willing to make the trek to support your local farmers, then your basic bitch card will be revoked. A farmers' market will gift you with everything you need at maximum freshness. You have no excuse, especially when you know the basket of veggies, herbs, and cheese will make a cute photo op after yoga class that will guarantee 100+ likes.

Arrange the tomatoes and burrata on a serving platter. Break open the burrata using a knife. Garnish with the basil leaves, drizzle with the olive oil and balsamic vinegar, and season with flaky salt and pepper. Serve.

Life-Affirming Gluten-Free Cheese Quesadillas

PREP TIME: 10 MINUTES   **COOK TIME:** 15 MINUTES
TOTAL TIME: 25 MINUTES   **YIELD:** 2 SERVINGS

Sometimes you want cheese, plain and simple. And sometimes you want to wrap said cheese in bread and dip it into sauces or sour cream so that it shines beyond its natural, glorious state. My grandma says that if she's not dead by ninety, she'll become a heroin addict, and I'm kind of like, #same, but swap heroin for cheese quesadillas. So simple, so satisfying, so something I can see myself making in bulk after losing a backgammon tournament at the nursing home.

1   First make the gluten-free tortillas: In a large bowl, whisk together the chickpea flour, tapioca flour, and salt until combined. Stream in the water and whisk until there are no lumps. Heat an 8-inch nonstick skillet over medium-high heat. Pour a generous ⅓ cup of the batter into the pan and swirl as you would if you were making a crepe. If necessary, spread the batter with a spatula to achieve an even layer all around the pan. Cook for 1 to 2 minutes per side, until the tortilla is golden brown. Remove from the heat and repeat with the remaining batter.

2   Grease the outside of 2 tortillas with ½ tablespoon of butter each. On the unbuttered side of one of the tortillas, spread the cream cheese. Top with the cheddar and Monterey Jack. Sandwich with the remaining tortilla, butter-side out. Place the quesadilla in a nonstick medium skillet over medium heat. Cook for 4 minutes per side, until the cheese is melted and the tortillas are golden brown and crispy. Remove from the skillet, cut into quarters, and serve with sour cream, guacamole, and salsa.

FOR THE GLUTEN-FREE TORTILLAS

¹/₂ cup chickpea flour
¹/₄ cup tapioca flour
¹/₂ teaspoon kosher salt
¹/₂ cup water

1 tablespoon unsalted butter
2 tablespoons whipped cream cheese
¹/₃ cup shredded sharp cheddar cheese
¹/₃ cup shredded Monterey Jack cheese
Sour cream, for serving
Guacamole, for serving
Salsa, for serving

JUST THE TIPS

If you don't have time to make your own gluten-free tortillas, you can always buy some. There are many options on the market, including quinoa flour tortillas, almond flour tortillas, brown rice tortillas, and coconut flour tortillas.

Everything Pigs in a Fluffy Down Comforter

PREP TIME: 25 MINUTES   **COOK TIME:** 1 HOUR 10 MINUTES
TOTAL TIME: 1 HOUR 50 MINUTES PLUS FREEZING
YIELD: 27 PIGS IN A BLANKET

One of my favorite anecdotes from my boss, Mary Gail Pezzimenti, is that she once slaved over an ultra-luxe and memorable dinner party for all of her friends, buying premium ingredients such as arctic char, filet mignon, and truffles. But at the end of the night, instead of pleading for the recipes to her expensive entrées, everyone asked how she made her pigs in a blanket. Insert crying-laughing emoji. Never underestimate the power of a crowd-pleaser, especially if served with gourmet dips and spreads that are just as easy to make or purchase as cocktail weiners wrapped in pastry dough. God bless America and God bless this everything variety with homemade bagel seasoning, caramelized onions, and all the money you won't be spending on ingredients that are difficult to pronounce and even more difficult to find in a standard grocery store.

FOR THE CARAMELIZED ONIONS

2 tablespoons olive oil

1 large yellow onion, peeled and thinly sliced

Kosher salt and freshly ground black pepper

FOR THE EVERYTHING BAGEL SEASONING

1 tablespoon white sesame seeds

1 tablespoon black sesame seeds

2 teaspoons poppy seeds

2 teaspoons minced garlic

2 teaspoons minced onion

1/2 teaspoon flaky sea salt

1 sheet frozen puff pastry, defrosted

3 tablespoons Dijon mustard

9 frankfurters

1 egg, beaten

2 tablespoons everything bagel seasoning

Honey Dijon mustard, for serving

JUST THE TIPS

These are great to make ahead. Freeze the pigs in a blanket on the sheet pan, wrapped in plastic wrap, then, once frozen, transfer to a zip-top bag and store in the freezer until you are ready to bake them, up to 2 months.

1   First make the caramelized onions: In a large nonstick skillet, heat the olive oil over medium-high heat. Add the onion and cook, stirring often, until tender, about 5 minutes. Reduce the heat to medium-low and cook, stirring occasionally, until the onions are caramelized, about 40 minutes. Season with salt and pepper and remove from the heat. Set aside to cool.

2   Meanwhile, make the everything bagel seasoning: Combine the white sesame seeds, black sesame seeds, poppy seeds, garlic, onion, and salt in a small bowl. (If not using immediately, store in an airtight container for up to 1 month.)

3   Line a baking sheet with parchment paper. On a lightly floured surface, roll out the puff pastry sheet to a 14-inch square. Cut it into nine 4½-inch squares. Brush the squares with 1 teaspoon of mustard each and top each with 1 tablespoon of the caramelized onions. (You can use any leftover onions for an omelet or to top a burger.) Top each square with a frankfurter and roll the puff pastry around the frankfurter, sealing the bottom. Brush the pastry with egg and sprinkle with the everything bagel seasoning. Cut each pastry-wrapped frankfurter into thirds on a bias and place on the prepared baking sheet. Freeze until firm, at least 1 hour (see tips).

4   Preheat the oven to 400°F.

5   Transfer the pigs in a blanket to the oven and bake for 20 to 25 minutes, until golden brown and puffed. Serve with the honey Dijon for dipping.

Take a Puff (Pastry)

It *is* possible to make your own puff pastry, but it's quite labor-intensive, requiring lots of folding and rolling out dough (this process creates the light, flaky layers). Luckily there is frozen store-bought puff pastry! When shopping, make sure to select all-butter puff pastry, such as Dufour. If you live near a Trader Joe's, they sell all-butter puff pastry as well.

When using frozen puff pastry, you need to plan ahead. Make sure to pull your puff pastry out of the freezer and allow it to defrost in the fridge overnight or at room temperature for 45 minutes to 1 hour.

Be careful not to roll puff pastry too thin, as it will not "puff" enough—and if there are any toppings (fruits, sauces, cheese), they will weigh down the pastry, so go easy on the amount.

Puff pastry loves a little egg wash before being baked. It will make the pastry golden and shiny.

Puff pastry can be used in both sweet and savory dishes, making it a versatile staple to have on hand. It can be used for appetizers, main courses, and desserts. Just a few ideas of what to make with puff pastry: potpies, pizzas, tarts, cheese straws, palmiers, tarte tatin, turnovers, and, of course, pigs in a blanket!

Puff pastry also makes entertaining easier. Many puff pastry recipes allow you to prep in advance and then throw your dish in the oven right before the party starts.

Sassy Shi-shit-o Peppers with Spicy Aioli

PREP TIME: 10 MINUTES **COOK TIME:** 5 MINUTES
TOTAL TIME: 15 MINUTES **YIELD:** 4 SERVINGS

I have an affinity for foods that are fun to say (such as jicama and bouillabaisse), which either makes me delightfully queer or a serious word nerd (both, probably). Shishito is on that list, perhaps because there is a vague profanity hidden in its name. But since one out of every ten to twenty of these peppers pack heat, you'll only strip out the "shi" and "o" part of the time. Otherwise, these blistered bad boys make an ideal appetizer for anyone craving a little crunch, green, and salt. They're also a great substitution for actual vegetables when you're in a pinch and steamed broccoli just isn't appealing for the 9,675th time.

FOR THE SPICY AIOLI

1/4 cup mayonnaise

1 tablespoon sriracha sauce

1 teaspoon soy sauce

2 teaspoons freshly squeezed lemon juice

1 clove garlic, minced

Kosher salt

2 teaspoons avocado oil

8 ounces shishito peppers (18 to 20 peppers)

1/2 medium lemon

Flaky sea salt

1 First make the spicy aioli: In a medium bowl, combine the mayonnaise, sriracha sauce, soy sauce, lemon juice, garlic, and salt.

2 In a large cast-iron skillet, heat the avocado oil over medium-high heat. Add the peppers in a single layer and char on both sides, 4 to 5 minutes. Remove from the skillet and transfer to a serving dish. Squeeze the juice from the lemon over the peppers and garnish with flaky salt. Serve with the spicy aioli for dipping.

THE MORE YOU GLOW
Avocado oil . . .

* Is rich in healthy fats such as oleic acid, a monounsaturated omega-9 fatty acid that is also a main component of olive oil.

* Has a high smoke point of approximately 520°F, making it a good option for high-heat cooking.

* Does not have a strong flavor profile. It's a good neutral oil.

The Master Cheese Ball Char-CUTE!-erie Board

PREP TIME: 15 MINUTES **COOK TIME:** 1 HOUR
TOTAL TIME: 1 HOUR 15 MINUTES
YIELD: 8 TO 10 SERVINGS

8 ounces cream cheese, softened

4 ounces feta cheese, crumbled

3 tablespoons grated Parmesan cheese

2 garlic cloves, minced

1 teaspoon hot sauce

1/4 cup chopped pimientos, drained

3/4 cup finely chopped pecans, toasted

3 tablespoons chopped fresh dill

3 tablespoons chopped fresh flat-leaf parsley

3 tablespoons chopped fresh chives

Kosher salt

Crackers, for serving

While I've always had a way with words, my artistic talents were quite . . . adorable, a term I frequently use in place of "tragic" or "awful." But like any basic bitch, I've always excelled at crafting and organizing, and charcuterie boards are an excellent way to show off my creativity and obsessive-compulsive personality. Literally everything has a spot around a cheese ball, and the accompanying dips, spreads, pickled vegetables, and finger foods are completely customizable to your preferences. I also set out a bottle of hand sanitizer, because frankly, you don't know where your friends' hands have been and it's not up to your taste buds to find out.

1   In the bowl of a stand mixer fitted with the paddle attachment, combine the cream cheese, feta, Parmesan, garlic, and hot sauce and beat to combine. Fold in the pimientos, pecans, and 1 tablespoon each of the dill, parsley, and chives. Taste and season with salt. Scrape the mixture onto a large piece of plastic wrap and form it into 1 large ball. Refrigerate to set for at least 1 hour.

2   Spread the remaining 2 tablespoons of each herb over a baking sheet. Roll the cheese ball in the herbs to coat, then transfer it to a serving plate. Serve with your favorite crackers.

JUST THE TIPS

Not interested in a single large cheese ball? You could also make 8 balls (2 ounces each) and serve them individually or as an addition to salads.

LITERALLY CAN'T EVEN

In addition to the crackers, crudités are a great option to serve alongside.

"I'm Not Boring, I'm Delicious!" Potato Salad

PREP TIME: 20 MINUTES **COOK TIME:** 20 MINUTES
TOTAL TIME: 4 HOURS 40 MINUTES **YIELD:** 8 SERVINGS

All hail the mighty potato, perhaps my favorite carb in the universe. There is nothing a potato can do wrong, and it obviously shines in salad form, too. This particular iteration, heavy on flavor, light on mushiness, will have everyone saying, "Can I have the recipe?" and not, "I think she got this tablecloth from the JOANN Fabrics sale bin." Some may argue that potato salad is boring and pointless—much like the time I liked every single one of Mariah Carey's photos on Instagram—but this hearty side is an American staple, and to dislike it is simply unpatriotic. Skladany 2020: Make America Love Potato Salad Again.

---

1 Put the potatoes in a large pot and cover with water. Season generously with salt. Bring to a boil over high heat, then reduce the heat to maintain a simmer. Cook until the potatoes are tender, 15 to 20 minutes. Drain and set aside to cool.

2 In a small bowl, combine the mayonnaise, sour cream, buttermilk, Dijon mustard, and whole-grain mustard. Season with salt and pepper. Set aside.

3 Cut the cooled potatoes into bite-size pieces, quarters, or halves and transfer to a large bowl. Add the celery, onion, dill, chives, and parsley. Pour the dressing over the salad and toss to coat. Taste and adjust the seasoning. Cover and refrigerate for at least 4 hours. Remove from the fridge and serve.

Ingredients

- 3 pounds small red and yellow potatoes
- Kosher salt
- $^1/_3$ cup mayonnaise
- $^1/_3$ cup sour cream
- $^1/_3$ cup buttermilk
- 2 tablespoons Dijon mustard
- 2 tablespoons whole-grain mustard
- Freshly ground black pepper
- $^3/_4$ cup finely chopped celery (about 2 stalks)
- $^1/_2$ cup finely chopped red onion ($^1/_2$ small onion)
- $^1/_3$ cup finely chopped fresh dill
- $^1/_4$ cup finely chopped fresh chives
- $^1/_4$ cup finely chopped fresh flat-leaf parsley

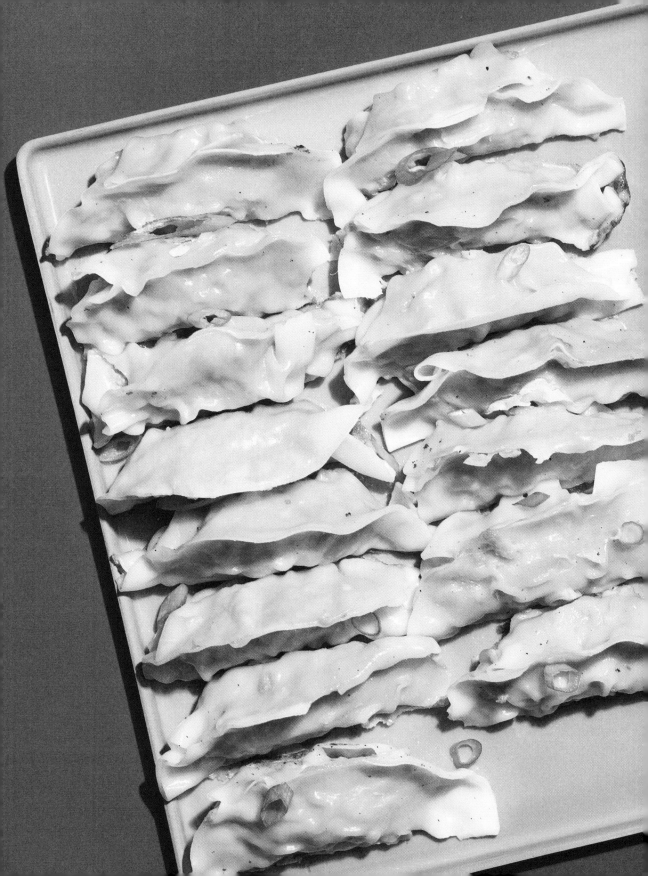

1 pound napa cabbage (about ¹/₂ head), finely chopped

1 tablespoon kosher salt

1 pound ground pork

2 tablespoons grated fresh ginger (from a 2-inch piece)

1 tablespoon minced garlic (about 4 cloves)

2 teaspoons sugar

³/₄ cup finely chopped scallions (4 or 5 large scallions)

¹/₄ cup finely chopped fresh cilantro leaves

2 tablespoons soy sauce

1 tablespoon toasted sesame oil

2 eggs, beaten

Kosher salt

60 round dumpling wrappers

Vegetable oil, for frying

FOR THE DIPPING SAUCE

2 tablespoons rice vinegar

¹/₄ cup soy sauce

1 teaspoon sugar

1 teaspoon toasted sesame oil

1 scallion (white and pale green parts only), finely chopped

¹/₄ teaspoon toasted sesame seeds

JUST THE TIPS

After seasoning your pork mixture, cook off a tablespoon in a sauté pan and give it a taste to make sure it is seasoned properly before forming all of your dumplings.

Once your dumplings are formed, you can freeze them in an airtight container for up to 3 months. Frozen dumplings take about twice as long to cook as fresh dumplings (6 to 8 minutes).

Pfft to Portion Control Pork Dumplings

PREP TIME: 1 HOUR   **COOK TIME:** 50 MINUTES
TOTAL TIME: 1 HOUR 50 MINUTES   **YIELD:** 55 TO 60 DUMPLINGS

Boys on Grindr looking for "friends" are like me walking into a Chinese restaurant and looking for bok choy. Lies and deceit. When I want dumplings, I want them bad. And like fries and sushi, I sometimes think dumplings are one of those foods that can carve an endless pit in my stomach. If they're cooked right and paired with a sweet-and-spicy sauce, I can keep going and going and the results are far from pretty. Have you ever seen a horse excitedly eat grain from a bucket? That horse is me, except with dumplings, so someone please put me out to pasture before my dreams of being on *My 600 lb. Life* (and becoming everyone else's problem) turn into a reality.

1   Make the pork dumplings: Place the cabbage in a bowl, sprinkle the salt evenly over it, and set aside for 15 minutes at room temperature. Wring out the excess water from the cabbage.

2   In a large bowl, combine the cabbage, pork, ginger, garlic, sugar, scallions, cilantro, soy sauce, sesame oil, and eggs. Season with salt and mix to combine.

3   Line two baking sheets with parchment paper. Fill a small bowl with water and set it nearby. On a clean work surface, lay out a few dumpling wrappers. Add a scant 1 tablespoon of the filling to each wrapper. Dip your finger in the water and dampen the edges of one wrapper. Starting from the right side, begin to pleat your dumpling. Pinch the corner to seal and then fold over a small flap, creating your first pleat; repeat as many or as few times as you'd like until you have sealed the dumpling. Use extra water if necessary to make sure the dumpling is sealed. Place the finished dumplings in rows on the prepared baking sheets. Repeat with the remaining filling and wrappers.

4   In a large nonstick skillet over medium heat, heat 1 tablespoon of vegetable oil. Add 8 to 10 dumplings to the pan at a time, making sure that they are not touching. Cook until the bottoms being to turn golden brown. Add a few tablespoons of water to the pan and cover with a lid. Reduce the heat to low and allow the dumplings to cook through, 3 to 5 minutes. Transfer to a platter. Repeat with the remaining dumplings, adding another tablespoon of oil to the pan before each batch.

5   Make the dipping sauce: In a medium bowl, combine the rice vinegar, soy sauce, sugar, sesame oil, scallion, and sesame seeds. Stir until the sugar dissolves. Serve with the dumplings.

Respectful Trail Mix

PREP TIME: 10 MINUTES   **COOK TIME:** 10 MINUTES
TOTAL TIME: 20 MINUTES   **YIELD:** 4¹/₄ CUPS

The person who invented the open-floor-plan office deserves each and every one of life's misfortunes. This also applies to the person who decides to eat trail mix in an open-floor-plan office. There is a time and a place for crunching, and three p.m. on a Thursday during literal crunch time is not ideal, Karen. And while my trail mix, chock-full of nuts, dried fruit, and chocolate, may be hard to resist, it's certainly more appreciated on a hike, during a walk through the park, or post–Barry's Bootcamp when your cringeworthy chewing noises can be masked by chirping birds and babbling brooks. Thank you in advance for attempting to not be an awful human.

1   Preheat the oven to 350°F.

2   In a medium bowl, toss the walnuts and cashews with a pinch of salt. Spread out evenly onto a baking sheet and bake for 10 minutes, until fragrant. Remove from the oven and let cool.

3   In a large bowl, toss together the cooled walnuts and cashews, almonds, pumpkin seeds, cherries, goji berries, apricots, dark chocolate chips, yogurt chips, and coconut flakes. Transfer to an airtight container and store at room temperature for up to 3 weeks.

³/₄ cup raw walnuts
¹/₂ cup raw cashews
Kosher salt
1 cup dry-roasted salted almonds
¹/₂ cup raw hulled pumpkin seeds (pepitas)
¹/₄ cup dried tart cherries
¹/₄ cup dried goji berries
¹/₄ cup dried apricots, chopped
¹/₄ cup dark chocolate chips
¹/₄ cup yogurt chips
¹/₄ cup unsweetened coconut flakes

JUST THE TIPS
Always lightly toast your raw nuts to bring out their flavor.

LITERALLY CAN'T EVEN
Customize your mix! Just follow the approximate ratio of 50 percent nuts, 30 percent dried fruit, 10 percent seeds, and 10 percent other, aka chocolates/candies/coconut.

Grand Entrance Entrées

Once you've mastered the art of appetizers, it's time to perfect your dinner party spread.

These recipes are tried-and-true dishes that are also—and most important—perfect for a Friday night in, when you'd rather save up for shoes than splurge on dinner. They're childhood staples, comfort foods, healthy and trendy concoctions, but all composed of high-quality ingredients that make you feel happy and satisfied. If you're anything like me (and you're reading this, I assume you are), you may need to lay down a tarp to ease the cleanup process. These plates will make you go hog wild and ditch any lessons in etiquette you learned in boarding school or from the movie *A Little Princess*. Consider yourself warned. There's no turning back.

3

I Can't Believe It's Not Unhealthy! Bowls on Bowls

Home is where the heart is, and also where my bodybuilder mother forces me to do a second cardio for the day. To counter my lack of endurance, I nourish my body with a plethora of healthy grain bowls after each and every workout. There are plenty of wholesome and organic grains (I'm a freak for freekeh) and meats to choose from, which means I never get sick of the flavor combinations. And when I'm attempting (and inevitably failing) to cut carbs, I simply swap out the grain for a green and proceed to cry about it not being quinoa, farro, or even wheat berries. Crying burns calories, right? At least I know my tears will provide some extra salty flavor, especially in a Hawaiian poke bowl with tuna. Delish.

Freekeh Grain Bowl

PREP TIME: 20 MINUTES   **COOK TIME:** 1 HOUR 30 MINUTES
TOTAL TIME: 1 HOUR 50 MINUTES   **YIELD:** 4 TO 6 SERVINGS

1   First make the oven-roasted cherry tomatoes: Preheat the oven to 300°F. In a large bowl, toss together the tomatoes, thyme, garlic, olive oil, and salt and pepper to taste. Spread the tomatoes over a baking sheet and roast for 1 hour 30 minutes, until the tomatoes begin to burst. Remove from the oven and let cool.

2   In a small pot, bring the water to a boil with a pinch of salt. Add the freekeh, reduce the heat to maintain a simmer, cover, and cook for 20 minutes, until almost all the water is absorbed. Turn off the heat and allow to sit for 10 minutes.

3   Meanwhile, in a large sauté pan over medium-high heat, heat the olive oil. Add the onion and cook until tender, about 6 minutes. Add the garlic and cook until fragrant, about 2 minutes. Add the corn and cook for 3 minutes. Remove from the heat and let cool.

4   Next, make the lemon vinaigrette: In a medium bowl, whisk together the lemon juice, vinegar, honey, and mustard to combine. Slowly add the olive oil while whisking the vinaigrette, then whisk until emulsified. Season with salt and pepper and set aside until ready to serve.

5   In a large bowl, toss together the roasted tomatoes, cooked freekeh, onion-corn mixture, pine nuts, goat cheese, parsley, and arugula. Season with salt and pepper and dress with the lemon vinaigrette.

FOR THE OVEN-ROASTED CHERRY TOMATOES

1 pint mixed cherry tomatoes

2 thyme sprigs

1 garlic clove, smashed

1 tablespoon olive oil

Kosher salt and freshly ground black pepper

$2^1/_2$ cups water

Kosher salt

1 cup cracked freekeh

2 tablespoons olive oil

1 large red onion, peeled and diced

2 garlic cloves, minced

$^3/_4$ cup corn (from 1 ear)

$^1/_4$ cup pine nuts, toasted

$^1/_2$ cup crumbled goat cheese

$^1/_2$ cup chopped fresh flat-leaf parsley

3 cups arugula

Freshly ground black pepper

FOR THE LEMON VINAIGRETTE

2 tablespoons freshly squeezed lemon juice (from 1 medium lemon)

2 tablespoons champagne vinegar

1 teaspoon honey

1 teaspoon Dijon mustard

$^1/_4$ cup olive oil

Kosher salt and freshly ground black pepper

THE MORE YOU GLOW

Freekeh is good for you in so many ways! It's made from green durum wheat that is high in fiber, calcium, zinc, and iron, and contains prebiotics to help regulate your digestive system. It can also assist in weight loss, thanks to the high protein and fiber content that keep you full longer.

FOR THE RICE

2 cups brown rice

2¹/₂ cups water

Pinch of kosher salt

2 tablespoons rice vinegar

1 tablespoon sugar

1 teaspoon kosher salt

FOR THE TUNA

2 tablespoons soy sauce

1 tablespoon rice vinegar

1 tablespoon sugar

2 tablespoons freshly squeezed lime juice (from 1 medium lime)

2 teaspoons toasted sesame oil

1 teaspoon grated fresh ginger (from a 1-inch piece)

¹/₂ teaspoon sambal oelek

3 scallions, white and light green parts only, thinly sliced

1 pound sashimi-grade ahi tuna, cut into bite-size pieces

¹/₂ cup English cucumber ribbons

¹/₂ cup thawed frozen shelled edamame

¹/₂ cup shredded carrots

¹/₄ cup sliced radishes

¹/₄ cup toasted white and black sesame seeds

JUST THE TIPS

Use only sashimi-grade tuna, and make sure it is fresh, not frozen. Freezing will compromise the texture of the fish. When purchasing the tuna, look for pieces without white streaks going through them. The white is connective tissue and is chewy and not desirable.

Poke Bowl

PREP TIME: 20 MINUTES   **COOK TIME:** 40 MINUTES
TOTAL TIME: 1 HOUR   **YIELD:** 4 SERVINGS

1   First make the rice: In a medium saucepot, bring the rice and water to a boil. Season with a pinch of salt. Cover, reduce the heat to a simmer, and cook for 30 minutes. Take off the heat, let the rice sit for 10 minutes, and then fluff with a fork. In a small bowl, combine the vinegar, sugar, and salt. Pour the vinegar mixture over the brown rice and toss to combine. Set aside until ready to use.

2   Meanwhile, make the tuna: In a large bowl, whisk together the soy sauce, vinegar, sugar, lime juice, sesame oil, ginger, sambal, and scallions. Add the tuna and toss to coat. Refrigerate to marinade at least 20 minutes and up to 1 hour.

3   Spoon the rice equally into four bowls. Add the tuna and garnish with the cucumber, edamame, carrots, radishes, and sesame seeds. Serve immediately.

Way-Too-Easy (If You Know What I Mean) One-Sheet-Pan Dinners

Life is busy and rough. Sometimes you just want to come home and make something quick and uncomplicated while *Little Women: Atlanta* plays in the background. Enter sheet-pan meals, a choose-your-own-adventure foray into cooking that isn't half as scary as a Goosebumps book (other than *Night of the Living Dummy*, of course). Through the helpful options that follow, you're able to pick your protein and vegetables, put them on a single baking sheet (no mess!), and bake it all for the same time at the same temperature. It's easier than *you* were at sorority formals in college. Just be sure to exercise safety. Things can get hot.

FOR THE SHEET PAN SALMON

- 1 pound small Yukon Gold potatoes, halved
- 1 pound Broccolini, ends trimmed
- 4 tablespoons olive oil
- Kosher salt and freshly ground black pepper
- 4 (5-ounce) skinless salmon fillets

FOR THE LEMON-DILL DRESSING

- 3 tablespoons freshly squeezed lemon juice (from 2 medium lemons)
- 2 tablespoons Dijon mustard
- 3 tablespoons olive oil
- 1 tablespoon chopped fresh dill
- 1 garlic clove, minced
- Kosher salt and freshly ground black pepper

Sheet Pan Salmon

PREP TIME: 15 MINUTES   **COOK TIME:** 30 MINUTES
TOTAL TIME: 45 MINUTES   **YIELD:** 4 SERVINGS EACH

1 Make the sheet pan salmon: Preheat the oven to 425°F. Line a baking sheet with foil.

2 Put the potatoes and Broccolini in a large bowl, drizzle with 2 tablespoons of the olive oil, and season with salt and pepper. Pour onto the prepared baking sheet in an even layer and roast for 15 minutes.

3 Meanwhile, drizzle the salmon with the remaining 2 tablespoons olive oil and season with salt and pepper. Add the salmon to the baking sheet with the potatoes and roast until the potatoes are tender and the salmon is almost cooked, 5 to 7 minutes more.

4 Meanwhile, make the lemon-dill dressing: In a medium bowl, combine the lemon juice, mustard, olive oil, dill, and garlic and season with salt and pepper. Set aside until ready to use.

5 Turn the oven to broil and brush the salmon and Broccolini with the lemon-dill dressing. Broil for 2 to 3 minutes, until the Broccolini is charred and the potatoes are crispy. Remove from the oven and serve.

Sheet Pan Chicken

PREP TIME: 15 MINUTES   **COOK TIME:** 30 MINUTES
TOTAL TIME: 45 MINUTES   **YIELD:** 4 SERVINGS

FOR THE GARLIC-AND-
HERB DRESSING

**4 tablespoons unsalted butter,
melted**

4 garlic cloves, minced

**2 teaspoons chopped fresh
thyme**

**2 teaspoons chopped fresh
rosemary**

**Kosher salt and freshly ground
black pepper**

FOR THE SHEET PAN
CHICKEN

**1 pound mixed baby potatoes,
halved (or quartered if large)**

4 tablespoons olive oil

**Kosher salt and freshly ground
black pepper**

**4 (5-ounce) boneless, skin-on
chicken breasts**

**1 pound thin asparagus, ends
trimmed**

Juice of ¹/₂ lemon

1   Preheat the oven to 425°F. Line a baking sheet with foil.

2   Make the garlic-and-herb dressing: In a medium bowl, combine the melted butter, garlic, thyme, and rosemary and season with salt and pepper. Set aside until ready to use.

3   Make the sheet pan chicken: In a large bowl, toss the potatoes with 2 tablespoons of the olive oil and season with salt and pepper. Spread them on half of the prepared baking sheet. Drizzle the chicken with the remaining 2 tablespoons olive oil and season with salt and pepper. Arrange the chicken on the same baking sheet and roast until the potatoes are tender, about 20 minutes.

4   Turn the oven to broil and remove the baking sheet. Add the asparagus and drizzle all with the garlic-and-herb dressing. Broil for 2 to 3 minutes until the asparagus is tender and the chicken is cooked through. Remove from the oven, stream the lemon juice over the top, and serve.

Sheet Pan Pork Tenderloin

PREP TIME: 15 MINUTES   **COOK TIME:** 30 MINUTES
TOTAL TIME: 45 MINUTES   **YIELD:** 4 SERVINGS EACH

1   Preheat the oven to 425°F. Line a baking sheet with foil.

2   Make the ginger-soy glaze: In a medium bowl, combine the soy sauce, vinegar, orange juice, brown sugar, sriracha sauce, sesame oil, ginger, and garlic. Mix until the sugar dissolves. Set aside.

3   Make the sheet pan pork tenderloin: In a large bowl, toss the carrots with 2 tablespoons of the vegetable oil and season with salt and pepper. Spread the carrots over the prepared baking sheet. Bake for 10 minutes.

4   Drizzle the pork tenderloin with the remaining 2 tablespoons vegetable oil and season with salt and pepper. Add the pork and the baby bok choy to the baking sheet with the carrots and drizzle everything with the ginger-soy glaze. Bake until the carrots and bok choy stems are tender and the pork is just about cooked through, about 15 minutes.

5   Turn the oven to broil. Broil for 2 to 3 minutes until the baby bok choy chars a bit. Remove from the oven and let rest for 10 minutes before serving.

FOR THE GINGER-SOY GLAZE

2 tablespoons soy sauce

2 tablespoons rice vinegar

1/4 cup freshly squeezed orange juice (from 1 orange)

2 tablespoons light brown sugar

1 tablespoon sriracha sauce

1 tablespoon toasted sesame oil

2 tablespoons grated fresh ginger (from a 2-inch piece)

2 garlic cloves, minced

FOR THE SHEET PAN PORK TENDERLOIN

1 pound carrots, peeled and sliced into 1 1/2-inch pieces on a bias

4 tablespoons vegetable oil

Kosher salt and freshly ground black pepper

1 (1-pound) pork tenderloin

1 pound baby bok choy (about 4 heads), halved

JUST THE TIPS

These dinners are made to mix and match. Pick your protein, pick your vegetables, add a starch and seasoning, and arrange it all on one sheet pan.

Looking to take the flavor up a notch? You can always marinate your proteins in advance. Pork and chicken can be marinated overnight. For seafood, especially if the marinade has an acidic ingredient in it, stick to no longer than 30 minutes.

A note about pork: It's a common fear that pork is undercooked if there's a little pink on the inside, but a little pink means the pork is *perfectly* cooked. You want to cook your pork to 145°F. Make sure to take carryover cooking into account when you allow the pork to rest.

"I Could Eat This, Like, Every Day" Sushi Rolls

PREP TIME: 45 MINUTES   **COOK TIME:** 30 MINUTES
TOTAL TIME: 1 HOUR 15 MINUTES   **YIELD:** 4 ROLLS EACH

Oh, sushi. My love for it knows no bounds. In fact, I am pretty sure I could eat it every day if there wasn't a legitimate fear of dying from mercury poisoning. I actually googled what mercury poisoning does to your body and it's like, not the worst way to go. Sure, you'll have some delayed motor skills and potential organ failure, but you get to eat sushi every day, so *meh*? I'm willing to take the risk, especially after realizing how easy it is to make within the comfort of my own closet-size Manhattan studio.

FOR THE SUSHI RICE

- ¹/₂ cup rice vinegar
- ¹/₄ cup sugar
- 2 tablespoons sake
- 2 cups short-grain sushi rice, rinsed well
- 2 cups water

FOR THE CALIFORNIA ROLL

- 2 sheets dark green nori seaweed, cut in half crosswise
- ¹/₃ cup toasted sesame seeds
- 4 sticks imitation crabmeat
- 1 avocado, thinly sliced
- 1 small seedless cucumber, julienned

FOR THE SPICY TUNA ROLL

- 8 ounces sashimi-grade tuna, cut into ¹/₄-inch cubes
- 3 tablespoons sriracha sauce
- 1 teaspoon toasted sesame oil
- 2 scallions, finely chopped
- ¹/₄ cup Japanese mayonnaise
- 2 sheets dark green nori seaweed, cut in half crosswise
- ¹/₄ cup toasted sesame seeds

TO SERVE

- Wasabi
- Pickled ginger
- Soy sauce

1. First make the sushi rice: In a small saucepan, heat the vinegar, sugar, and sake just until the sugar dissolves. Remove from the heat and allow to cool to room temperature.

2. Place the rinsed rice in a rice cooker with the water. Cook according to the manufacturer's directions for sushi rice. Transfer the cooked rice to a large bowl. Pour the vinegar-sake mixture over the rice and fold to ensure the rice is evenly coated. Let sit for 10 minutes, covered with a warm, damp towel to keep warm.

3. Make the California roll: Cover a sushi mat with plastic wrap. Place a sheet of nori on the sushi mat. Add ½ to ¾ cup of the sushi rice and spread it evenly over the nori. Sprinkle with a quarter of the sesame seeds. Flip the nori over so the rice is facing the sushi mat and is lined up with the bottom edge of the mat.

4. On the bottom third of the nori, add 1 stick of the imitation crabmeat and one quarter each of the avocado and cucumber. Using your fingers to hold the filling in place, pull up on the sushi mat and begin to roll until your nori sheet becomes a cylinder. Remove the sushi mat and, using a very sharp knife, cut the roll crosswise into 6 equal portions. Repeat with the remaining ingredients to make 3 more rolls.

5. Make the spicy tuna roll: In a medium bowl, combine the tuna, 2 tablespoons of the sriracha sauce, the sesame oil, and the scallions. Mix to combine and keep chilled until ready to use.

6. In a small bowl, combine the Japanese mayonnaise and the remaining 1 tablespoon sriracha sauce. Set the spicy mayo aside until ready to use.

7   Cover the sushi mat with plastic wrap. Place a sheet of nori on the sushi mat. Add ½ to ¾ cup of the sushi rice and spread it evenly over the nori. Sprinkle with a quarter of the sesame seeds. Flip the nori over so the rice is facing the sushi mat and is lined up with the bottom edge of the mat.

8   On the bottom third of the nori, add a quarter of the tuna in a line. Using your fingers to hold the tuna in place, pull up on the sushi mat and begin to roll until your nori sheet becomes a cylinder. Remove the sushi mat and, using a very sharp knife, cut the roll crosswise into 6 equal portions. Add a dollop of spicy mayo to the top of each roll. Repeat with the remaining ingredients to make 3 more rolls.

9   Serve with wasabi, pickled ginger, and soy sauce.

BASIC BASICS

The vinegar-sake mixture you add to the sushi rice is called *awase-zu*.

Sashimi is an assortment of thinly sliced raw fish without rice.

Nigiri is a style of sushi where the fish is placed on top of a pillow of rice; not to be confused with classic sushi rolls.

Maki is a type of roll where the seaweed wrap is on the outside.

Rolls are when the rice is on the outside and the seaweed is wrapped inside.

Traditionally, you should never mix your wasabi and soy sauce unless you're eating sashimi.

The pickled ginger is used as a palate cleanser, not as an additional topping for your sushi.

JUST THE TIPS

It is *very* important to wash your rice before cooking it. If you don't, the rice will be too sticky and become a ball. You will know it's ready when the water runs clear.

Don't cook your rice on the stovetop. You should use a rice cooker for your sushi rice to achieve the right consistency.

You will need a bamboo rolling mat to make sushi. Pro tip: Carefully wrap your bamboo mat in plastic wrap to avoid getting sushi rice stuck in it.

A Deeply Personal Cauliflower Pizza

PREP TIME: 25 MINUTES **COOK TIME:** 30 MINUTES
TOTAL TIME: 55 MINUTES **YIELD:** 1 (10-INCH) PIZZA

Every time I'm pitched cauliflower-something by a publicist, an angel loses its wings. It's like people who vape or get their septum pierced: We get it, it's a thing, congratulations, but stop telling us about it every day of our lives. Cauliflower crust definitely makes personal pizzas healthier, but it's similar to those times when I say I'm going on a five-mile jog and am back ten minutes later. The intentions are there, though the self-sabotage is real. So enjoy this pizza however you prefer. If you opt for the surprisingly delicious cauliflower crust below, that's great! But just know that you're probably going to top it with processed meat and cheese anyway. It's pizza, and your diet should be reserved for less amazing things, like dandelion-green salads and cayenne–lemon juice elixirs.

1 Preheat the oven to 425°F. Line a baking sheet with parchment paper.

2 First make your crust: Put the cauliflower rice in a microwave-safe large bowl and cover. Microwave on high for 6 to 8 minutes, until tender. Uncover and allow to cool slightly.

3 Once the cauliflower has cooled, transfer it to a kitchen towel and wring out the excess moisture. Return it to the large bowl. Add the Parmesan, mozzarella, oregano, basil, garlic powder, salt, and egg. Mix to combine. Transfer to the prepared baking sheet and press into a 10-inch circle. Bake the crust for 15 minutes, until golden.

4 Remove from the oven and top with the tomato sauce and mozzarella. Return the pizza to the oven and bake until the cheese is melted and bubbling, about 5 minutes. Remove from the oven and, if desired, garnish with basil, red pepper flakes, and Parmesan. Slice and serve.

FOR THE CAULIFLOWER CRUST

3 cups riced cauliflower (from 1 large head cauliflower)

1/4 cup freshly grated Parmesan cheese

1 cup freshly grated mozzarella cheese (about 4 ounces)

1/2 teaspoon dried oregano

1/2 teaspoon dried basil

1/2 teaspoon garlic powder

3/4 teaspoon kosher salt

1 egg, lightly beaten

TOPPINGS

1/3 cup tomato sauce

1/2 cup freshly grated mozzarella cheese

Fresh basil leaves, for garnish (optional)

Red pepper flakes, for garnish (optional)

Parmesan cheese, grated, for garnish (optional)

BASIC BASICS

You can also cook your cauliflower rice in the oven. Spread it over a baking sheet and bake for 15 minutes until tender. Let it cool and then wring out any excess moisture.

Grilled Cheese with Cheesy Fries, aka Rock Bottom

PREP TIME: 20 MINUTES **COOK TIME:** 25 MINUTES
TOTAL TIME: 45 MINUTES **YIELD:** 4 SERVINGS

When life seems to punch you in the ribs when you're already down, it's time to put cheese on more cheese and call it a day. Also, fries are my favorite food in the whole world, so you can put pretty much anything on them and I'll eat them. This list may or may not include garlic aioli, hot sauce, gochujang, chocolate syrup, gravy, and an unidentifiable mystery sauce that I once grabbed at a county fair (let's just say that I should be #sponsored by Pepto-Bismol after that one). But cheese is good . . . cheese is great . . . and any melted variety makes it a fantastic excuse to forget about life's hardships as you drizzle it on fried potatoes and establish a thematic extension to your very basic, albeit very satisfying, grilled cheese sandwich.

1 Preheat the oven to 200°F. Line a baking sheet with a wire rack.

2 First make the cheesy fries: Fill a large Dutch oven with 4 inches of canola oil and heat the oil to 325°F. Add the potato sticks, in batches if necessary, and cook for 6 minutes, until tender and just beginning to color. Transfer to the prepared baking sheet and increase the temperature of the oil to 350°F. Return the sticks to the hot oil for their second fry and cook for 1 to 2 minutes, until golden brown. Transfer to the baking sheet and season generously with salt. Keep warm in the oven until ready to serve.

3 In a medium saucepot, toss the shredded cheese with the cornstarch. Add the evaporated milk. Cook over medium-high heat, stirring occasionally, until the cheese has melted. Add the hot sauce, ketchup, and a pinch of salt and stir to combine. Remove from the heat. Serve with or over your fries.

4 Make the grilled cheese: Lay out the slices of bread on a clean surface. Spread one side of each slice with 1½ teaspoons of the mayonnaise. Put the Parmesan on a plate and dip the mayonnaise side of the bread in the Parmesan. Lay the bread Parmesan-side down on your work surface. Spread 2 of the slices with the apricot jam and the other 2 slices with the mustard, dividing them evenly. Top each slice evenly with the cheddar and fontina and sandwich shut.

5 Coat a large nonstick sauté pan with cooking spray. Heat over medium heat and add the sandwiches. Cook until the Parmesan has turned golden and crisp, 2 to 3 minutes per side. Serve.

FOR THE CHEESY FRIES
Canola oil, for frying

2 medium russet potatoes (about 1 pound), cut into ⅓-inch sticks

Kosher salt

8 ounces yellow cheddar cheese, shredded (2½ cups)

1 tablespoon cornstarch

1 (12-ounce) can evaporated milk

1 tablespoon hot sauce (such as Frank's RedHot)

1 tablespoon ketchup

FOR THE GRILLED CHEESE
4 slices Pullman bread

2 tablespoons mayonnaise

¾ cup freshly grated Parmesan cheese

2 tablespoons apricot jam

4 teaspoons Dijon mustard

4 slices sharp white cheddar cheese

½ cup shredded fontina cheese

JUST THE TIPS
Looking for a shortcut? Buy frozen bagged French fries. I won't tell.

LITERALLY CAN'T EVEN
Feel free to mix up the cheeses: fontina, American, cheddar, Gruyère, triple crème Brie, goat cheese, Pecorino Romano, or any of your favorites.

Add-ins are always welcome in grilled cheese sandwiches. Try tomato, green apple, bacon, arugula, or avocado. Or experiment with other condiments such as tomato jam, pesto, or harissa.

FOR THE "CHASHU" BRAISED PORK BELLY

1¹/₂ pounds boneless skin-on pork belly

2 tablespoons sugar

Kosher salt and freshly ground black pepper

1 cup sake

FOR THE CHICKEN DASHI

1 tablespoon mirin

¹/₄ cup soy sauce

1 tablespoon sake

8 cups chicken stock

2 cups water

20 dried shiitake mushrooms

1 head garlic, cut in half horizontally

1 (2-inch) piece fresh ginger, sliced thick

1 (12-inch) sheet kombu seaweed

1 cup bonito flakes

4 eggs

1 pound fresh ramen noodles

¹/₂ cup sliced scallions (optional)

Chili-garlic sauce

1 lime, cut into wedges

2 sheets nori seaweed, cut in half

JUST THE TIPS

Always cook your ramen noodles in boiling water just before serving. Avoid cooking in the broth, as this can result in gummy noodles. If you can't find fresh noodles, you can substitute dried.

After braising, chilling the pork belly overnight in the refrigerator allows for easy slicing.

BASIC BASICS

Dashi is a clear broth made with kombu seaweed and bonito flakes.

Tare is "the soul of ramen," a flavored soy sauce.

Chashu is braised pork belly.

It's Raining Ramen

PREP TIME: 40 MINUTES   **COOK TIME:** 2 HOURS
TOTAL TIME: 2 HOURS 40 MINUTES PLUS CHILLING OVERNIGHT
YIELD: 4 SERVINGS

There's nothing I crave more on a rainy day or when I'm feeling sick than ramen. And since I'm sick literally every week, I crave ramen a lot. Whether it's the heat, the salt and spice of the broth, the complexities of flavors, or the laundry list of ingredients, it always comes together to create a harmoniously decadent dish that temporarily cures any cold symptoms or irrational fears of contracting an STD. Miracle food? Yes, but don't expect me not to slurp on this as if I just got massive lip injections and am sipping from a garden hose. It's meant to be messy, especially for Americans who can't master foreign utensils.

1   Preheat the oven to 350°F.

2   First make the "chashu" braised pork belly: Put the pork belly in a baking dish. Sprinkle with the sugar and season with salt and pepper. Pour the sake over the pork belly and roast for 2 hours, flipping halfway through, until the pork is tender and beginning to caramelize. Remove from the oven and let the pork belly cool in its remaining braising liquid to room temperature. Transfer to the refrigerator to chill overnight.

3   To make the chicken dashi: Combine the mirin, soy sauce, and sake in a small bowl. Set aside.

4   In a large pot, combine the chicken stock, water, shiitake mushrooms, garlic, ginger, kombu, and bonito flakes. Bring to a boil, then reduce the heat to maintain a simmer and cook until the liquid has reduced by roughly 25 percent, about 1 hour. Strain the broth and add the mirin mixture. Keep warm until serving.

5   Bring a medium saucepot of water to a boil. Add the eggs, reduce the heat to maintain a low simmer, and cook for 6 minutes, until soft-boiled. Remove the eggs and run them under cold water. Peel the eggs, slice in half, and set aside.

6   Bring a large pot of salted water to a boil. Add the ramen noodles and stir, making sure they do not stick. Cook for 1 minute. Drain.

7   To serve, remove the pork belly from the fridge and thickly slice it. Divide the noodles among four bowls and ladle in the chicken dashi. Top with the braised pork belly, eggs, scallions (if using), chili-garlic sauce, and a lime wedge. Tuck half of a sheet of nori along the side of the bowl and serve.

I Like Big Buns and I Cannot Lie Burgers with Sweet Potato Fries

PREP TIME: 30 MINUTES **COOK TIME:** 35 MINUTES
TOTAL TIME: 1 HOUR 5 MINUTES **YIELD:** 4 BURGERS

If there was a job that required me to stay at home and play *The Sims* or *RollerCoaster Tycoon* all day, I'd quit my day job yesterday. I guess I could also live with being a taste tester for cheeseburgers and fries. Is there really anything better than the famous diner duo? No, there isn't. And if you disagree, then you also probably like shoestring fries, which are by far the most disappointing side dish ever created. How the hell are you supposed to dip a pile of straggly potatoes into honey mustard? You're not.

FOR THE SWEET POTATO FRIES

1 pound sweet potatoes, peeled and cut into ¹/₂-inch-thick sticks

2 tablespoons avocado oil

1 tablespoon cornstarch

Kosher salt

FOR THE BURGERS

¹/₂ pound ground brisket

¹/₂ pound ground short rib

¹/₂ pound ground sirloin

Kosher salt and freshly ground black pepper

8 slices yellow American cheese

4 brioche burger buns, toasted

Caramelized onions (see page 70), for serving

Tomatoes slices, for serving

Pickle slices, for serving

Green leaf lettuce, for serving

Mayonnaise, for serving

Ketchup, for serving

JUST THE TIPS

Ask your butcher for the ground brisket, short rib, and sirloin. If you are having trouble sourcing the ground meats, you can always use 1¹/₂ pounds 80% lean ground beef.

1 First make the sweet potato fries: Preheat the oven to 450°F with two baking sheets inside.

2 In a large bowl, toss the sweet potato sticks with the avocado oil, cornstarch, and salt to taste. Spread out evenly between the two preheated baking sheets. Bake until golden brown and cooked through, about 30 minutes, flipping halfway through. Remove from the oven and transfer to a platter.

3 Meanwhile, make the burgers: Heat a grill to medium-high or heat a grill pan over medium-high heat.

4 In a large bowl, combine the ground brisket, short rib, and sirloin. Form it into four 6-ounce patties. Season the burgers generously with salt and pepper. Grill, uncovered, for 2 to 3 minutes. Flip and top each burger with 2 slices of cheese, then cook for an additional 2 minutes, until the cheese has melted and the burgers are cooked to medium-rare. Remove from the grill.

5 To serve, put a burger on the bottom of a toasted bun. Stack caramelized onions, tomatoes, pickles, and lettuce on the burger. Add mayonnaise and/or ketchup to the top bun, if desired, and close the burger. Repeat with the remaining ingredients. Serve with the sweet potato fries.

Black Bean–Quinoa Burger

PREP TIME: 45 MINUTES   **COOK TIME:** 30 MINUTES
TOTAL TIME: 1 HOUR 15 MINUTES   **YIELD:** 6 BURGERS

1 Preheat the oven to 400°F. Line a baking sheet with parchment paper.

2 Put the black beans in a large bowl and, using a potato masher, mash until blended, with some larger pieces of beans remaining. Set aside.

3 In a large sauté pan over medium-high heat, heat the olive oil. Add the bell pepper and onion. Sauté until softened, about 7 minutes. Add the garlic and cook for 1 minute, until fragrant. Add the cumin, chili powder, and paprika and cook for an additional minute. Remove from the heat and transfer to the bowl with the black beans. Add the Worcestershire sauce, quinoa, panko, and eggs and season with salt and black pepper. Mix to combine.

4 Divide the bean mixture into six 6-ounce portions and form them into patties and place on the prepared baking sheet. Bake until the outside is crispy, about 20 minutes, flipping halfway through. During the last 5 minutes of cooking, add a cheese slice to the top of each patty.

5 Meanwhile, make the special sauce: Combine the mayonnaise, ketchup, sriracha, pickles, Worcestershire sauce, and salt and pepper to taste in a small bowl. Set aside.

6 To serve, spread some special sauce on the bottom and top of each toasted bun. Place a black bean patty on the bottom bun. Add tomato slices and arugula. Cap with the bun top and serve.

THE MORE YOU GLOW

Just because there is no meat in these burgers doesn't mean they aren't filled with protein. Both black beans and quinoa are jam-packed with the stuff, helping to keep you full long after you finish this burger.

FOR THE BURGER

- 2 (14.5-ounce) cans black beans, drained and rinsed
- 2 tablespoons olive oil
- 1 red bell pepper, finely chopped
- 1 small red onion, finely chopped
- 4 garlic cloves, minced
- 2 teaspoons ground cumin
- 2 teaspoons chipotle chili powder
- $1/2$ teaspoon hot smoked paprika
- 2 tablespoons Worcestershire sauce
- 1 cup cooked quinoa
- $1/2$ cup panko bread crumbs
- 2 eggs
- Kosher salt and freshly ground black pepper
- 6 slices yellow cheddar cheese

FOR THE SPECIAL SAUCE

- $1/2$ cup mayonnaise
- 2 tablespoons ketchup
- 1 tablespoon sriracha sauce
- $1/4$ cup finely chopped dill pickles
- 1 tablespoon Worcestershire sauce
- Kosher salt and freshly ground black pepper

- 6 potato buns, toasted, for serving
- Tomato, sliced, for serving
- Arugula, for serving

JUST THE TIPS

Use two lids from quart containers (lined with plastic wrap) to form the perfect burger!

Sexy Slaw That Just Happens to Be Served on Fish Tacos

PREP TIME: 30 MINUTES   **COOK TIME:** 15 MINUTES
TOTAL TIME: 45 MINUTES   **YIELD:** 4 TO 6 SERVINGS

Summer may be defined by watermelon, grilling, and sweating through the $25 kaftan you bought on Amazon, but for me, it's all about fish tacos. And the slaw. That delightfully cold and crisp slaw that I crave in my dreams between all of the insomnia and Klonopin-induced REM cycles. Some things are meant to be together, unlike Britney Spears and Kevin Federline, and slaw was made to top a lightly battered fish that is fried to perfection. Please also pile on the cilantro, because I'm not a monster human who trashes such an herbal delicacy and blames it on genetics.

1   First make the cabbage slaw: In a medium bowl, toss together the cabbage, carrots, scallions, lime juice, sugar, and salt to taste. Let sit until ready to serve.

2   Make the fish: Fill a large Dutch oven with about 3 inches of canola oil and heat the oil to 350°F. Line a baking sheet with a wire rack.

3   In a large bowl, combine 2½ cups of the flour, 1 teaspoon of the salt, the baking powder, chili powder, and Mexican beer. Mix to form a batter. In another bowl, combine the remaining 1½ cups flour and 1 teaspoon salt. Season the halibut with salt and pepper. Dredge the halibut pieces in the flour mixture and then dip in the batter to coat. Add a few pieces at a time to the hot oil and cook until golden brown and cooked through, about 5 minutes. Transfer to the prepared baking sheet and repeat with the remaining pieces of fish.

4   Meanwhile, make the chipotle crema: In a medium bowl, combine the mayonnaise, crema, lime juice, adobo sauce, and salt to taste. Set aside.

5   To assemble, divide the fried fish among the tortillas. Top with the slaw, pico de gallo, chipotle crema, and cilantro leaves. Serve.

LITERALLY CAN'T EVEN
Can't find halibut? Any other flaky white fish will do;
think flounder, snapper, mahi-mahi, grouper, or cod.

FOR THE CABBAGE SLAW
**3 cups shredded napa cabbage
(1 small head)**
**1 cup shredded carrots
(1 to 2 medium)**
**1 cup thinly sliced scallions
(about 4)**
**3 tablespoons freshly
squeezed lime juice
(from 1 medium lime)**
1 teaspoon sugar
Kosher salt

FOR THE FISH
Canola oil, for frying
4 cups all-purpose flour
**2 teaspoons kosher salt, plus
more for seasoning**
2 teaspoons baking powder
1 teaspoon chili powder
2½ cups dark Mexican beer
**2 pounds skinless halibut,
cut into 1-inch-thick strips**
Freshly ground black pepper

FOR THE CHIPOTLE CREMA
⅓ cup mayonnaise
⅔ cup crema
**2 tablespoons freshly
squeezed lime juice
(from 1 medium lime)**
3 tablespoons adobo sauce
Kosher salt

6 flour tortillas, warmed
Pico de gallo, for serving
Cilantro leaves, for serving

Bully-Proof Bacon-Wrapped Mini Meat Loaves

PREP TIME: 35 MINUTES   **COOK TIME:** 40 MINUTES
TOTAL TIME: 1 HOUR 15 MINUTES   **YIELD:** 4 MINI-MEAT LOAVES

- ¹/₄ cup plus 3 tablespoons ketchup
- 2 tablespoons light brown sugar
- 1 tablespoon apple cider vinegar
- 12 slices bacon
- 1 large shallot, finely chopped
- 2 garlic cloves, minced
- ¹/₄ cup chopped fresh flat-leaf parsley
- ¹/₄ cup freshly grated Pecorino Romano cheese
- ¹/₂ cup panko bread crumbs
- 1 egg, beaten
- 1 teaspoon Worcestershire sauce
- ¹/₂ pound ground sirloin
- ¹/₂ pound ground chuck
- Kosher salt and freshly ground black pepper
- 4 ounces yellow cheddar cheese, cut into ¹/₂-inch cubes

JUST THE TIPS

To ensure your meat loaf isn't dry, you want to use a high-fat meat (something with at least 15% fat).

Make sure not to overmix your meat mixture; that will make it dry and dense.

Cook off a small portion of the meat mixture in a sauté pan and taste it to make sure the seasonings are to your liking.

Yes, bacon is still a thing. It's like how I have twenty-two shows I want to stream but find myself watching *The Lion King* for the three hundredth time because I know it will always deliver. Bacon is *The Lion King*—it never fails us, especially when used to wrap things that would otherwise be boring or even repulsive. In this case, it's meat loaf, because meat on meat can mean only good things, and greasy pork will elevate *anything*, even if that anything was served during lunch in the middle school cafeteria during prime bullying hour. Sure, I may be scarred from the chants of mean kids who grew up to live in their parents' basements, but I always had meat loaf on my side. And now I have a bacon-wrapped meat loaf on my side that childhood bullies can read about from their parents' basements. Ah, the circle of life.

1   Preheat the oven to 400°F. Line two baking sheets with parchment paper.

2   In a small bowl, whisk together ¼ cup of the ketchup, the light brown sugar, and the vinegar until blended. Set aside.

3   Arrange the bacon slices on one of the prepared baking sheets in a single layer, leaving space between them. Bake for 10 to 12 minutes, until the edges are just slightly crisp but the bacon is still flexible. Remove from the oven and set aside; keep the oven on.

4   In a large bowl, combine the shallot, garlic, parsley, pecorino, panko, egg, 3 tablespoons ketchup, the Worcestershire sauce, ground sirloin, and ground chuck. Mix to combine and season with salt and pepper. Divide the mixture evenly into four 6-ounce portions and shape them into logs, 5 inches long by 2 inches wide. Use your thumb to make a small well in the center of the logs and place 1 ounce of the cheese cubes in each well. Form the meat mixture back into logs, completely enclosing the cheese.

5   Brush the meat loaves with the prepared glaze, wrap 3 slices of bacon around each log, and place on the second prepared baking sheet. Bake for 20 to 25 minutes, until cooked through. Remove from the oven and allow to rest for 15 minutes before serving.

Polar Vortex Chili

PREP TIME: 20 MINUTES   **COOK TIME:** 45 MINUTES
TOTAL TIME: 1 HOUR 5 MINUTES   **YIELD:** 4 TO 6 SERVINGS

2 tablespoons olive oil

1 large red onion, diced

2 garlic cloves, minced

1 small red bell pepper, cored and diced

1 small yellow bell pepper, cored and diced

1 medium sweet potato, peeled and diced into ³/₄-inch cubes

1 canned chipotle pepper in adobo sauce, finely chopped

1 tablespoon ground cumin

1 tablespoon chipotle chili powder

1 teaspoon cayenne

¹/₄ teaspoon hot smoked paprika

Kosher salt and freshly ground black pepper

2 (15.5-ounce) cans diced fire-roasted tomatoes with green chilies

1 (15.5-ounce) can black beans, drained and rinsed

1 cup vegetable broth

Juice of 1 medium lime

TOPPINGS

1 avocado, sliced

Leaves from 1 bunch cilantro

Crema

Grated yellow cheddar cheese

Pickled red onions (see page 114)

1 lime, cut into wedges

I've avoided grocery store shopping before major snowstorms and found myself stuck only with the cat treats I'd accidentally ordered online because I'd mistaken them for jerky. Oops. When I'm smart enough to gather ingredients and actually prepare a dish in advance, my favorite hibernation recipe is chili. But a very specific type of chili, with chipotle powder and sweet potatoes. I love a smoky-and-sweet balance to offset the jar of cayenne that I'm inevitably going to drop into the slow cooker. This is, perhaps, the only food that can make offensively cold weather even temporarily acceptable, which is saying a lot, because this Florida boy hates cold weather more than being out past midnight.

1   In a medium Dutch oven over medium-high heat, heat the olive oil. Add the red onion and cook until translucent, about 5 minutes. Add the garlic, red and yellow bell peppers, and sweet potato and cook until the peppers are softened, about 4 minutes. Add the chipotle in adobo sauce, cumin, chili powder, cayenne, and paprika. Season with salt and black pepper. Stir to combine.

2   Add the tomatoes, beans, and broth. Bring to a boil, then reduce the heat to maintain a simmer, cover, and cook for 30 minutes, until the sweet potato is tender. Add the lime juice, taste, and adjust the seasonings to your liking.

3   Serve with your desired toppings.

Study Buddy Broccoli-Cheddar Soup in a Bread Bowl

PREP TIME: 15 MINUTES   **COOK TIME:** 40 MINUTES
TOTAL TIME: 55 MINUTES   **YIELD:** 4 TO 6 SERVINGS

Project Cozy, commence! Surrender to the idea that even though it's a Friday night, you're just not going out. Sure, your hair is curled and your foundation is set, but it's snowing (at least in your mind) and it's best for you to change into pajamas, sit this one out, and write that memoir or depressing poetry you've been thinking about for months. To do this successfully, all you need is every basic bitch's favorite "study food": broccoli-cheddar soup in a carb-laden bread bowl. It's about the same number of calories as those twelve vodka-soda-splash-of-cranberries you were planning to down anyway, but with far fewer sexual consequences. So slurp up and embrace some creative productivity. You may just make winter a little less awful.

1. In a large Dutch oven over medium-high heat, melt the butter. Add the onion and garlic and cook until translucent, about 5 minutes. Add the celery and cook for 2 more minutes, until it begins to soften. Add the flour and cook for 2 minutes. Slowly whisk in the chicken stock to combine. Add the half-and-half, milk, and nutmeg. Season with salt and pepper and bring to a simmer. Reduce the heat and cook, uncovered, stirring occasionally, until the soup thickens, about 10 minutes.

2. Add the broccoli and carrot and cook until the vegetables are tender, stirring occasionally, about 20 minutes. Transfer 2 cups of the soup to a blender and puree until smooth. Return the blended portion to the Dutch oven and stir to combine. Add the cheese and stir until it melts. Remove from the heat. Taste and adjust the seasoning, if necessary.

3. To serve, ladle into bread bowls, if using, or soup bowls.

5 tablespoons unsalted butter

1 small yellow onion, finely chopped

2 garlic cloves, minced

1 stalk celery, finely diced

$1/4$ cup all-purpose flour

2 cups chicken stock

1 cup half-and-half

1 cup whole milk

$1/4$ teaspoon freshly grated nutmeg

Kosher salt and freshly ground black pepper

3 cups finely chopped broccoli florets (about 1 head)

1 large carrot, peeled and julienned

8 ounces yellow cheddar cheese, shredded ($2^1/2$ cups)

4 mini round sourdough bread boules, hollowed out, leaving a 1-inch border (optional)

LITERALLY CAN'T EVEN

Most of the time you can swap out fresh vegetables for frozen (defrosted, of course), but for this recipe I highly recommend using fresh broccoli to achieve the best results.

Individual bread bowls are a fun option for serving this soup. However, if you can't find mini boules, you can always serve the soup in bowls with a nice piece of crusty bread on the side for dipping.

Tender AF Filet Mignon with Crispy AF Brussels Sprouts

PREP TIME: 15 MINUTES   **COOK TIME:** 35 MINUTES
TOTAL TIME: 50 MINUTES   **YIELD:** 2 SERVINGS

If your idea of cooking beef is to recite a Hail Mary and hope for the best, then whoa, that cow died in vain, and hi, I'm here to ensure you never mess this one up again. Filets can be surprisingly easy if you master the sear and pray your smoke detector doesn't go off in the process. Pair your protein with crispy Brussels sprouts, because *duh*, and you'll have yourself a well-rounded meal that earns an adulting seal of approval. Just be sure to put your cheap red wine in a sippy cup since you're also prone to spilling.

FOR THE CRISPY BRUSSELS SPROUTS

³/₄ pound Brussels sprouts, trimmed and halved

2 tablespoons olive oil

Pinch of red pepper flakes

Kosher salt and freshly ground black pepper

2 tablespoons freshly grated Parmesan cheese

Zest of ¹/₂ medium lemon

2 (6-ounce) filet mignon steaks, at room temperature

Kosher salt and freshly ground black pepper

2 tablespoons olive oil

4 tablespoons unsalted butter

1 small shallot, minced

³/₄ cup red wine

2 thyme sprigs

1   Preheat the oven to 400°F.

2   First start the crispy Brussels sprouts: In a large bowl, toss the Brussels sprouts with the olive oil and red pepper flakes, and season with salt and black pepper. Pour onto a baking sheet and spread into an even layer. Roast for 20 minutes, until tender. Increase the oven temperature to 450°F and roast for an additional 5 minutes, until crispy. Remove from the oven and transfer to a serving dish; keep the oven on. Sprinkle the Parmesan and lemon zest over the top.

3   While the Brussels sprouts are roasting, season the steaks generously with salt and pepper. In a medium cast-iron skillet, heat 1 tablespoon of the olive oil over medium-high heat. Add the steaks and sear for 2 minutes on each side. Top each steak with 1 tablespoon of the butter and transfer the skillet to the oven. Cook for 4 minutes, until the internal temperature reaches 125°F for a medium-rare steak. Remove from the oven, transfer the steaks to a cutting board, and tent with foil. Let rest for 10 minutes.

4   Heat the same cast-iron skillet over medium-high heat. Add the remaining 1 tablespoon olive oil and the shallot and sauté until the shallot is tender, about 4 minutes. Add the wine and thyme and cook until the wine has reduced by half. Add the remaining 2 tablespoons butter and swirl to melt. Remove the thyme sprigs and discard. Season the sauce with salt and pepper.

5   Serve the red wine–shallot sauce over the rested filets mignons with the crispy Brussels sprouts on the side.

Not De-Pressed BLTini

PREP TIME: 30 MINUTES **COOK TIME:** 1 HOUR
TOTAL TIME: 1 HOUR 30 MINUTES **YIELD:** 4 TO 6 SERVINGS

Bikinis, martinis, crostinis, and paninis. Why are there so many basic bitch staples that end in "ini"? The good thing is that you don't have to say "eeny meeny miny moe" to any of the above—a basic bitch can have it all. If the only thing you've recently pressed is an acrylic nail from Sally's, get excited for this pressed BLTini on sourdough bread with extra mayo and emphasis on the B. Because like that L'Oréal model with the annoyingly perfect and shiny hair in that commercial you just saw, you may just be worth it.

FOR THE PICKLED RED ONIONS

1¹/₂ cups distilled white vinegar

1¹/₂ cups water

¹/₄ cup granulated sugar

1 tablespoon kosher salt

2 tablespoons mustard seeds

2 tablespoons coriander seeds

1 tablespoon black peppercorns

2 garlic cloves, thinly sliced

¹/₂ teaspoon red pepper flakes

2 bay leaves

2 large red onions, thinly sliced

FOR THE ROASTED TOMATO JAM

1¹/₂ pounds Roma tomatoes (about 6 large)

2 tablespoons olive oil

Kosher salt and freshly ground black pepper

1 tablespoon butter

1 small yellow onion, finely diced

2 garlic cloves, minced

1 tablespoon light brown sugar

Pinch of red pepper flakes

1 tablespoon sherry vinegar

1 First make the pickled red onions: In a medium saucepot, combine the distilled white vinegar, water, sugar, salt, mustard seeds, coriander seeds, peppercorns, garlic, red pepper flakes, and bay leaves. Bring to a boil, then reduce the heat and simmer until the sugar and salt have dissolved. Put the onions in a large glass bowl. Pour the pickling liquid over the onions and let sit until cooled to room temperature. Transfer into airtight containers and store in the refrigerator until ready to use, up to 1 month.

2 Next make the roasted tomato jam: Preheat the oven to 450°F. Line a baking sheet with a silicone baking mat. Cut the tomatoes in half lengthwise and remove the core. Drizzle with the olive oil and season with salt and pepper. Place the tomatoes cut-side down on the prepared baking sheet and roast for about 25 minutes, until they are very soft, have some color to them, and have cooked down. Remove from the oven and let cool, then discard the tomato skins. Reduce the oven temperature to 350°F.

3 Meanwhile, in a straight-sided medium skillet over medium-high heat, melt the butter. Add the onion and garlic and cook until translucent, about 5 minutes. Add the roasted tomatoes, light brown sugar, and red pepper flakes. Break up the tomatoes with a wooden spoon until they have a slightly chunky consistency. Simmer the tomatoes until they have achieved a jam-like texture, about 20 minutes. Add the sherry vinegar and season with salt and black pepper. Remove from the heat and let cool completely.

4 Meanwhile, make the herbed mayonnaise: In a medium bowl, combine the mayonnaise, lemon juice, tarragon, parsley, and chives. Season with salt and pepper. Set aside.

5 Make the BLTini: Divide the bacon between two baking sheets and bake for 15 to 20 minutes, until crispy. Remove from the oven and drain the bacon on paper towels.

6 Preheat a panini press. In a medium bowl, toss the arugula with the olive oil and season with salt and pepper. Set aside.

7 Spread the cut side of one half of the baguette with the tomato jam. Add the bacon, overlapping as necessary, then the pickled red onions and arugula. Spread the cut side of the other half of the baguette with the herbed mayonnaise and close the baguette. Cut into 4 to 6 sandwiches and brush with the melted butter. Cook the sandwiches in batches on the panini press until golden. Serve.

JUST THE TIPS

Extra tomato jam will last in an airtight container in the refrigerator for about 2 weeks.

If you don't own a panini press, you can wrap your sandwiches in foil and grill for 3 minutes on each side. Just be sure to press down on them with a spatula as they cook.

FOR THE HERBED MAYONNAISE

1/2 cup mayonnaise

2 tablespoons freshly squeezed lemon juice (from 1 medium lemon)

1 tablespoon finely chopped fresh tarragon

1 tablespoon finely chopped fresh flat-leaf parsley

1 tablespoon finely chopped fresh chives

Kosher salt and freshly ground black pepper

FOR THE BLTINI

1 pound thick-cut bacon

2 cups baby arugula

1 tablespoon olive oil

Kosher salt and freshly ground black pepper

1 baguette, sliced in half lengthwise

1 tablespoon unsalted butter, melted

Anti–Shopping Mall Orange Chicken Stir-Fry

PREP TIME: 20 MINUTES **COOK TIME:** 30 MINUTES
TOTAL TIME: 50 MINUTES **YIELD:** 4 TO 6 SERVINGS

- ¹/₄ cup low-sodium soy sauce
- 1 tablespoon orange zest
- ³/₄ cup freshly squeezed orange juice (from about 3 oranges)
- ¹/₃ cup light brown sugar
- 1 tablespoon toasted sesame oil
- 2 tablespoons minced fresh ginger
- 3 garlic cloves, minced
- ¹/₄ to ¹/₂ teaspoon red pepper flakes
- 2 scallions, sliced
- 1 tablespoon rice vinegar
- ¹/₂ cup water
- 2 tablespoons cornstarch
- 4 tablespoons olive oil
- 1 small red onion, peeled and thinly sliced
- 1 red bell pepper, cored and sliced into ¹/₂-inch-thick strips
- 3 cups broccoli florets (from 1 head)
- 1 pound boneless, skinless chicken breasts, sliced into ¹/₂-inch-thick strips
- Kosher salt and freshly ground black pepper
- 1 cup snow peas, strings removed and sliced in half on a bias
- Cooked white or brown rice, for serving (optional)
- Toasted sesame seeds, for garnish

I can't believe malls are still a thing. I mean, I know they're not as big of a thing as they used to be (thank you, Internet), but who actually enjoys visiting public places with hordes of loud and obnoxious people dressed in what are essentially pajamas with tattered tennis shoes? As someone whose favorite thing in the world is when passengers get shushed in the quiet car, that person is not me. Though I'll certainly make an exception for "loud and obnoxious" when it comes to orange chicken samples served aggressively on toothpicks. But when even this gets annoying and tiresome and simply not worth the trek to the burbs, here's a recipe that anyone can make within the confines of their home.

1 In a medium bowl, whisk together the soy sauce, orange zest, orange juice, and light brown sugar. In a small sauté pan over medium heat, combine the sesame oil, ginger, and garlic. Cook until fragrant, 2 minutes. Add the red pepper flakes, scallions, rice vinegar, and the soy sauce mixture and bring to a simmer. In a small bowl, whisk together the water and cornstarch. Pour the cornstarch mixture into the orange sauce, reduce the heat to low, and simmer until thickened, about 3 minutes. Remove from the heat.

2 In a large nonstick skillet over medium-high heat, heat 2 tablespoons of the olive oil. Add the onion and the bell pepper. Cook until the onion is translucent, about 5 minutes. Add the broccoli and cook for 4 minutes, until tender. Transfer the vegetables to a large bowl. Season the chicken with salt and pepper. Heat the remaining 2 tablespoons olive oil in the same skillet, then add the chicken. Cook until the chicken is cooked through, about 5 minutes. Add the snow peas, orange sauce, and cooked vegetables. Simmer until the snow peas are tender, about 2 minutes. Serve over rice, if desired, and garnish with toasted sesame seeds.

LITERALLY CAN'T EVEN
Not a fan of chicken? You can substitute many different proteins for it, including beef, pork, or even tofu.

FOR THE HOMEMADE RANCH DRESSING

¹/₄ cup mayonnaise

¹/₄ cup sour cream

¹/₃ cup buttermilk

1 tablespoon apple cider vinegar

¹/₂ teaspoon onion powder

1 garlic clove, minced

1 tablespoon chopped fresh dill

1 tablespoon chopped fresh chives

1 tablespoon chopped fresh flat-leaf parsley

Kosher salt and freshly ground black pepper

FOR THE SALADS

Kosher salt

2 boneless, skinless chicken breasts

2 tablespoons olive oil

8 slices extra-thick-cut bacon

4 eggs

1 pint cherry tomatoes, halved

2 avocados, chopped

4 Persian cucumbers, sliced

¹/₂ cup crumbled blue cheese

4 cups chopped romaine lettuce (from 2 heads)

1 cup chopped butter lettuce (from 1 head)

JUST THE TIPS

Short on time? You can always buy a precooked rotisserie chicken and hard-boiled eggs to cut down on the prep.

The avocado is layered at the bottom of the mason jar so that it can be coated in some of the dressing. If you are preparing in advance, you can always toss your avocado in a little lemon juice to prevent browning.

Widemouth mason jars work best for salads. You have a little bit more room at the top to reach all of the ingredients.

"I'm So Artisanal!" Cobb Mason Jar Salad with Homemade Ranch Dressing

PREP TIME: 20 MINUTES   **COOK TIME:** 45 MINUTES
TOTAL TIME: 1 HOUR 5 MINUTES   **YIELD:** 4 QUART-SIZE MASON JAR SALADS

Literally every summer day in NYC before work: "Oh, I'm looking so cute today." Upon arrival: "Does anyone have a paper bag I can cinch over my head?" On days like these when I have to rely strictly on personality to get by, I'm just happy to find anything adorable to get me through the day. And with a mason jar salad, that adorable thing just happens to be my desk-side lunch. Don't expect to keep the Weight Watchers points down with this one, though. It's piled high with a homemade ranch dressing that will have you wishing your waistline were hidden and not the famous valley.

1   Preheat the oven to 350°F.

2   First make the homemade ranch dressing: In a medium bowl, combine the mayonnaise, sour cream, buttermilk, vinegar, onion powder, garlic, dill, chives, and parsley. Season with salt and pepper. Set aside.

3   Make the salads: Fill a medium bowl with lukewarm water, then add two generous pinches of salt and the chicken breasts. Allow them to brine for 15 minutes. Remove from the brine, rinse with cold water, and pat dry. Place the chicken breasts on a baking sheet and brush with the olive oil. Place the bacon on a second baking sheet and transfer both pans to the oven. Bake until the internal temperature of the chicken reaches 165°F and the bacon is crispy, 20 to 25 minutes. Remove from the oven and allow to rest for 10 minutes. Cut both the chicken and bacon into ¹/₂-inch cubes and set aside to cool.

4   Meanwhile, place the eggs in a medium saucepot, add water to cover, and bring to a boil. When the water reaches a boil, reduce the heat to barely a simmer and cook for 8 minutes. Prepare an ice bath in a large bowl. Remove the pot from the heat and add the eggs to the ice bath; let sit for 5 minutes. Remove the shells and chop the eggs.

5   To assemble, put 2 to 3 tablespoons of the dressing at the bottom of each of four 1-quart mason jar, depending on how much dressing you like on your salad. Divide the ingredients evenly among the jars, layering the tomatoes, avocados, cucumbers, chicken, bacon, hard-boiled egg, blue cheese, and romaine and butter lettuces. Seal the jars with their lids and refrigerate. When ready to serve, shake the jar to coat the salad in the dressing, remove the lid, and enjoy.

Totes About Tots
Tuna Fish Casserole

PREP TIME: 40 MINUTES   **COOK TIME:** 1 HOUR
TOTAL TIME: 1 HOUR 40 MINUTES   **YIELD:** 6 TO 8 SERVINGS

I'm not entirely sure what makes the tater tot so basic bitch, other than it being a cutesy finger food that you can easily dip in ketchup and toss into your mouth. There was a girl in my second-grade class who used to hoard her tots during lunch, only to pick at them with an ugly manicure and seemingly torture those of us who finished within thirty seconds of sitting down. This casserole is clearly not for her and, frankly, it's not for anyone who can't handle a spatula full of the grated potatoey goodness that we've come to accept as a meal. I dedicate this recipe to my second-grade self. You now live in a world with endless tater tots right at your beautiful fingertips. Enjoy!

1   Preheat the oven to 425°F.

2   First make the cream of mushroom soup: In a medium braiser, heat the olive oil and butter over medium-high heat until melted. Add the mushrooms and cook until browned, about 5 minutes. Add the leek and cook for 4 minutes, until translucent. Add the garlic and thyme and cook for 1 minute, until fragrant. Stir in the flour and allow the raw flour flavor to cook out, about 1 minute. Add the vegetable broth slowly, stirring to combine. Season with salt and pepper. Bring to a simmer and cook for 10 minutes, stirring occasionally.

3   Stir in the half-and-half and Marsala. Taste and adjust the seasoning, if necessary. Remove from the heat and allow to cool slightly. Discard the thyme bundle. Transfer to a blender and blend until smooth. Pour the soup back into the braiser.

4   Make the casserole: Add the spinach to the soup and mix to combine, breaking up any large clumps of spinach. Slightly break up the tuna fillets by hand and add to the top of the mushroom soup. Top with the cheese and layer the tater tots in concentric circles around the top of the dish. Bake for 35 minutes, until the tater tots are crispy and golden brown. Remove from the oven and allow to cool for 10 minutes before serving.

FOR THE CREAM OF MUSHROOM SOUP

1 tablespoon olive oil

2 tablespoons unsalted butter

1 pound cremini mushrooms, cut into small dice

1 leek, cut into small dice (about ³/₄ cup)

2 garlic cloves, minced

6 fresh thyme sprigs, tied with butcher's twine

2 tablespoons all-purpose flour

2 cups vegetable broth

Kosher salt and freshly ground black pepper

¹/₂ cup half-and-half

2 tablespoons dry Marsala wine

FOR THE CASSEROLE

2 (10-ounce) boxes frozen chopped spinach, thawed and drained of excess water

1 (6.7-ounce) jar tuna fillets in olive oil, drained

3 ounces Colby Jack cheese, grated (1 cup)

1 (28-ounce) package frozen extra-crispy tater tots

JUST THE TIPS

If you don't have a braiser, feel free to use a 12-inch cast-iron pan.

Oodles of Noodles, Balls, and a Sauce for Every Season

If you're a gay man and ever want to feel really bad about yourself, just go on Tinder in Italy. If you're an Italian American and think you know how to cook pasta, just go to a restaurant in Italy. Basically, Italy makes me hate myself, but you can hate yourself a little less with these recipes, tailored to your very specific personal preferences. Working on a six-pack? Go for zoodles. Is your alcohol intake so extreme that it needs to be in your food? There's a vodka sauce for that. Just dumped a man and convinced that calories are your only soul mate? Alfredo, baby. And don't forget the meatballs. There's a ball for everyone, girlfriend. Two, if you're lucky.

Two-Noods and Three-Meat Balls

PREP TIME: 25 MINUTES **COOK TIME:** 1 HOUR
TOTAL TIME: 1 HOUR 25 MINUTES **YIELD:** 6 TO 8 SERVINGS

1 First make the pomodoro sauce: In a medium Dutch oven, heat the olive oil over medium-high heat. Add the onion and garlic and cook until translucent, about 5 minutes. Add the red pepper flakes and tomato paste and cook for 30 seconds. Tie the oregano and thyme sprigs with butcher's twine and add the herb bundle to the pot with the tomatoes. Season with salt and black pepper. Bring to a boil, then reduce the heat to maintain a simmer and cook for 20 minutes.

2 Meanwhile, make the ricotta meatballs: Heat a small nonstick sauté pan over medium-high heat. Add the olive oil, onion, and garlic and cook until translucent, about 5 minutes. Remove from the heat and let cool.

3 In a large bowl, combine the ground beef, veal, and pork, the ricotta, Parmesan, nutmeg, panko, egg, parsley, and cooled onion mixture. Season with salt and pepper. Be sure not to overmix. Fry off a small portion of the meat mixture to taste for seasoning. Using an ice cream scoop, scoop about 20 meatballs onto a baking sheet.

4 Add the meatballs to the simmering pomodoro sauce, cover, and cook for 20 minutes, until cooked through. Remove the meatballs from the sauce and keep warm.

5 Bring a large pot of salted water to a boil. Cook the spaghetti until al dente according to package directions. Drain.

6 Meanwhile, add the zucchini noodles to the pomodoro sauce and cook until al dente, about 5 minutes. Add the cooked spaghetti to the sauce and mix to combine.

7 Serve the spaghetti and zucchini noodles topped with the meatballs. Garnish with Parmesan and basil.

JUST THE TIPS

If you can't find zucchini noodles at the store, spiralize 1 large zucchini before you make the meatballs and set aside.

You don't have to mix spaghetti with zucchini noodles. This is just a clever way to sneak in vegetables, since the two ingredients have similar textures.

If you'd prefer to bake your meatballs, put them on baking sheets lined with parchment paper and bake in a preheated 400°F oven for about 20 minutes, until golden brown and cooked through.

FOR THE POMODORO SAUCE

2 tablespoons olive oil
1 small red onion, finely diced
4 garlic cloves, minced
Pinch of red pepper flakes
1 tablespoon tomato paste
2 fresh oregano sprigs
2 fresh thyme sprigs
2 (28-ounce) cans whole peeled tomatoes, crushed by hand
Kosher salt and freshly ground black pepper

FOR THE RICOTTA MEATBALLS

2 tablespoons olive oil
1 small yellow onion, finely diced
2 garlic cloves, minced
$^1/_2$ pound ground beef
$^1/_2$ pound ground veal
$^1/_2$ pound ground pork
$1^1/_4$ cups whole-milk ricotta cheese
$^3/_4$ cup finely grated Parmesan cheese
$^1/_2$ teaspoon freshly grated nutmeg
$^1/_2$ cup panko bread crumbs
1 egg, beaten
$^1/_2$ cup finely chopped fresh flat-leaf parsley
Kosher salt and freshly ground black pepper

8 ounces spaghetti
8 ounces zucchini noodles (from 1 large zucchini)
Freshly grated Parmesan cheese, for serving
Chopped fresh basil, for garnish

Ingredients (Meatless Eggplant "Meatballs")

5 tablespoons olive oil

1 small yellow onion, finely diced

2 garlic cloves, minced

1 medium/large eggplant, peeled and finely diced (about 6 cups)

Kosher salt

2 teaspoons finely chopped fresh oregano

2 teaspoons finely chopped fresh basil, plus more for serving

$^1/_2$ cup vegetable broth

$^3/_4$ cup all-purpose flour

1 cup plain bread crumbs

2 eggs, beaten

3 ounces Pecorino Romano, grated (1 cup), plus more for serving

$^1/_2$ cup chopped fresh flat-leaf parsley

Freshly ground black pepper

Avocado oil, for frying

Meatless Eggplant "Meatballs"

PREP TIME: 35 MINUTES   **COOK TIME:** 45 MINUTES
TOTAL TIME: 1 HOUR 20 MINUTES   **YIELD:** 6 TO 8 SERVINGS

1 Heat the olive oil in a large sauté pan over medium heat. Add the onion and garlic and cook until translucent, about 5 minutes. Add the eggplant and season with salt. Cook until softened and browned, about 10 minutes. Add the oregano, basil, and vegetable broth. Bring to a simmer and cook until the liquid has evaporated, about 10 minutes. Using a potato masher, mash the eggplant until it forms a paste. Transfer to a large bowl to cool.

2 Once cooled, add $^1/_4$ cup of the flour, the bread crumbs, eggs, Pecorino Romano, and parsley. Season with salt and pepper. Using an ice cream scoop, divide the mixture into 35 balls and place on a baking sheet. Transfer to the freezer to chill for 20 minutes.

3 Put the remaining $^1/_2$ cup flour in a small baking dish. Dredge the meatballs in the flour. Fill a small Dutch oven with 1 inch of avocado oil and heat over medium-high heat. Set a wire rack on a baking sheet. Add the meatballs to the hot oil in batches and fry until golden brown, about 5 minutes. Transfer to the rack and repeat to fry the remaining meatballs. Season with salt and sprinkle with more pecorino and chopped basil.

JUST THE TIPS

These meatballs can be eaten as an entrée but are also delicious as an appetizer, served on a small spoon with some pomodoro sauce (see page 121) and a garnish of Pecorino Romano cheese and basil.

1 stick unsalted butter

$^1/_2$ cup heavy cream

Kosher salt and freshly ground black pepper

6 ounces Parmesan cheese, freshly grated (about 2 cups)

Alfredo Sauce

PREP TIME: 5 MINUTES   **COOK TIME:** 10 MINUTES
TOTAL TIME: 15 MINUTES   **YIELD:** ABOUT 1$^3/_4$ CUPS

In a straight-sided large skillet over medium-high heat, combine the butter and cream and cook until the butter melts. Season with salt and pepper. Add the Parmesan and stir until the cheese has melted and the sauce comes together. Toss with your desired pasta to combine. Make sure to reserve some of the pasta cooking water to thin out the sauce and keep it smooth and creamy.

Pesto Sauce

PREP TIME: 5 MINUTES **COOK TIME:** 5 MINUTES
TOTAL TIME: 10 MINUTES **YIELD:** ABOUT 1 CUP

- **1/3 cup pine nuts**
- **2 garlic cloves**
- **4 cups fresh basil leaves**
- **1/2 cup olive oil**
- **1/2 cup grated Parmesan cheese**
- **1 tablespoon freshly squeezed lemon juice (from 1 small lemon)**
- **Kosher salt**

In a food processor, pulse the pine nuts and garlic until finely chopped. Add the basil and olive oil and process until a paste forms. Add the cheese and lemon juice, and season with salt. Process until smooth.

JUST THE TIPS

Pesto is a great sauce to prepare and keep in your freezer for last-minute pesto needs. Just make sure to store it in an airtight container with a glug of olive oil on top (this keeps the surface from oxidizing). Press some plastic wrap on top of the olive oil and seal the container. Store in the freezer for up to 6 months.

The lemon juice brightens the pesto sauce. If you aren't a fan or would rather have a traditional pesto, leave the lemon juice out.

Vodka Sauce

PREP TIME: 5 MINUTES **COOK TIME:** 15 MINUTES
TOTAL TIME: 20 MINUTES **YIELD:** 6 TO 8 SERVINGS

- **4 cups pomodoro sauce (see page 121) or jarred sauce**
- **1 cup vodka**
- **1/2 cup heavy cream**
- **Cooked pasta, for serving**
- **Freshly grated Parmesan cheese, for serving**

In a straight-sided large skillet over medium-high heat, combine the pomodoro sauce and the vodka and simmer until the sauce has reduced by 25 percent, about 15 minutes. Stir in the cream and reduce the heat to low. Cook until the cream is incorporated and the sauce is heated through. Serve with pasta and garnish with Parmesan.

JUST THE TIPS

Vodka sauce also freezes great. Store it in an airtight container, or if you are low on space, you can portion the sauce into freezer zip-top bags. Vodka sauce will last in the freezer for up to 6 months. It's good practice to label and date your freezer items so you know what the contents are and if you are using them within the correct amount of time.

Ingredients

1 cup dried red lentils

4 cups tomato sauce

Pinch of red pepper flakes

15 lasagna noodles (from a 1-pound box)

1 (16-ounce) package extra-firm tofu, drained

2 garlic cloves

¼ cup nutritional yeast

⅓ cup oat milk

2 tablespoons olive oil

2 tablespoons freshly squeezed lemon juice (from 1 medium lemon)

½ teaspoon freshly grated nutmeg

2 (10-ounce) packages frozen chopped spinach, thawed and drained

Kosher salt and freshly ground black pepper

¼ cup fresh basil leaves, julienned

THE MORE YOU GLOW

To up the protein in the lasagna, I added red lentils. Red lentils have 24 grams of protein per 1 cup cooked. They break down in the sauce and are nearly undetectable.

Tofu acts as a great "faux" ricotta in this lasagna. It is also a great source of protein, with 37 grams per pound.

A Vegan's Favorite Vegan Lasagna with Vegan Tofu

PREP TIME: 30 MINUTES   **COOK TIME:** 50 MINUTES
TOTAL TIME: 1 HOUR 20 MINUTES   **YIELD:** 8 TO 10 SERVINGS

Aw-wee-oo! Killer tofu! Okay, so this lasagna may not actually kill you, but the taste is killer. In fact, I'm pretty sure that Doug Funnie would approve. (Even if it doesn't contain mayonnaise. Ba-dum-bump.) The best part about it is that it's vegan, which means you get to talk about being vegan for hours on end, just like every other vegan you know. So let's give your vegan friends another excuse to hijack the conversation by preparing and bringing over this vegan lasagna. #VeganLife.

1   Preheat the oven to 350°F.

2   Bring a medium saucepot of salted water to a boil over high heat. Add the lentils and cook until tender, about 15 minutes. Drain and return to the saucepot. Add the tomato sauce and red pepper flakes. Simmer for 5 minutes, until the lentils begin to break down. Remove from the heat and set aside.

3   Bring a large pot of salted water to a boil over high heat. Add the lasagna noodles and cook until al dente, 2 to 3 minutes less than the package instructions. Drain and set aside in a single layer so they do not stick together.

4   In a food processor, combine the tofu, garlic, nutritional yeast, oat milk, olive oil, lemon juice, and nutmeg. Process until smooth and the consistency resembles ricotta cheese. Transfer to a large bowl and add the spinach. Season with salt and pepper and mix to combine.

5   To assemble, spread a thin layer of the tomato sauce over the bottom of a 9 x 13-inch baking dish. Top with 5 lasagna noodles, slightly overlapping them. Add half of the tofu mixture and top with a layer of noodles. Add a layer of sauce and repeat, ending with a layer of noodles covered with a layer of sauce. Cover the baking dish with foil and bake for about 20 minutes, until the lasagna is bubbling. Remove the foil and bake for an additional 10 minutes. Remove from the oven and allow to cool for at least 20 minutes before serving. Garnish with the basil, slice, and serve.

JUST THE TIPS

If you're craving a little bit more "cheese," you can always add nondairy mozzarella to the layers.

Slow Cooker Pork Dive Bar

PREP TIME: 25 MINUTES   **COOK TIME:** 5 HOURS
TOTAL TIME: 5 HOURS 25 MINUTES   **YIELD:** 6 TO 8 SERVINGS

I don't think an open buffet has ever made money off of a Skladany, so a DIY buffet situation scares me to my infrequently visible core. But if you're cooking for people with normal-size appetites, these slow cooker recipes can be a great excuse to gather the besties, make skinny margaritas, and throw a midweek fiesta. It's also an excellent excuse to use up all the pork that you bought at Costco during last week's shopping high (and subsequent blackout because of the free samples) and have absolutely no idea what to do with. A true win-win, if you ask me.

1   First make the chipotle BBQ pork: In a multicooker, combine the onion, oregano, bay leaves, chipotle pepper, adobo sauce, ketchup, vinegar, and crushed tomatoes. Season the boneless pork shoulder on all sides with salt and black pepper. Add the pork shoulder to the sauce mixture and turn to coat. Secure the lid and set to slow cook on high for 5 hours or on low for 8 hours.

2   Transfer the pork from the multicooker to a large bowl and allow to cool slightly. Meanwhile, turn the multicooker to cook and reduce the liquid by half until it has thickened slightly. Using two forks, shred the meat, discarding any fatty sections, and return it to the thickened sauce. Taste and adjust the seasoning, if necessary.

3   Meanwhile, make the coleslaw: In a medium bowl, combine the napa cabbage, red cabbage, carrot, and scallions. In a small bowl, combine the celery seed, mayonnaise, and vinegar. Season with salt and pepper. Before serving, toss the cabbage mixture with the mayo sauce.

4   Using tongs to drain off some of the liquid, add a heaping mound of the chipotle BBQ pork to a toasted bun. Top with some pickled red onions and coleslaw. Serve.

FOR THE CHIPOTLE BBQ PORK

1 medium yellow onion, diced

1 teaspoon dried oregano

2 bay leaves

1 small canned chipotle pepper in adobo sauce, minced (seeds removed for less spice, if you want), plus 1 1/2 teaspoons adobo sauce from the can

3/4 cup ketchup

1/4 cup apple cider vinegar

1 (14.5-ounce) can crushed tomatoes

1 (3-pound) boneless pork shoulder, trimmed of fat

Kosher salt and freshly ground black pepper

FOR THE COLESLAW

4 cups thinly sliced napa cabbage

1 cup thinly sliced red cabbage

1 large carrot, grated

4 scallions, thinly sliced

1/2 teaspoon celery seed

1/2 cup mayonnaise

2 tablespoons apple cider vinegar

Kosher salt and freshly ground black pepper

Sandwich buns, toasted

Pickled red onions (see page 114)

FOR THE MEXICAN SPICE BLEND

2 tablespoons chili powder

2 tablespoons light brown sugar

2 teaspoons ground cumin

1 1/2 teaspoons ground coriander

1/2 teaspoon cayenne pepper

1 teaspoon smoked paprika

1 teaspoon ground oregano

1 teaspoon onion powder

1 teaspoon garlic powder

FOR THE MEXICAN PULLED PORK

3 pounds boneless pork shoulder, trimmed of excess fat

Kosher salt and freshly ground black pepper

2 tablespoons olive oil

1/2 cup chicken stock

FOR THE PEPPERS AND ONIONS

1 tablespoon olive oil

1 large Vidalia onion, sliced 1/4 inch thick

1 red bell pepper, sliced 1/4 inch thick

1 orange bell pepper, sliced 1/4 inch thick

Kosher salt and freshly ground black pepper

Slow Cooker Mexican Pork Fajitas

PREP TIME: 40 MINUTES   **COOK TIME:** 5 HOURS 20 MINUTES
TOTAL TIME: 6 HOURS   **YIELD:** 6 TO 8 SERVINGS

1   Make the Mexican spice blend: In a medium bowl, combine the chili powder, light brown sugar, cumin, coriander, cayenne, paprika, oregano, onion powder, and garlic powder.

2   Make the Mexican pulled pork: Season the pork generously with salt and pepper and rub all over with 2 tablespoons of the Mexican spice blend. Add the olive oil to a multicooker and set it to the cook function. Once the oil has heated, add the pork and brown on all sides until golden, 3 to 4 minutes per side. Add the chicken stock. Cover. Switch the function to slow cook and cook on high for 5 hours or on low for 8 hours, until the pork is fork tender.

3   Transfer the pork from the multicooker to a large bowl. Allow to cool slightly. Pour the liquid from the multicooker into a separate bowl. Shred the pork with two forks, discarding any excess fat. Add the reserved liquid a little at a time to moisten the pork. Taste and adjust the seasoning, if necessary. Keep warm until ready to serve.

4   Next, make the peppers and onions: Set the multicooker to the cook function. Add the olive oil, onion, and bell peppers. Cook until the vegetables are tender and slightly charred, 10 minutes. Season with salt and black pepper. Transfer to a serving platter.

5   Meanwhile, make the chipotle-lime crema: In a blender, combine the sour cream, chipotle, lime juice, olive oil, honey, cilantro, and salt. Blend on low until combined. Transfer to a serving bowl and refrigerate until ready to serve.

6   Make the charred corn salad: Heat a grill to medium-high or heat a grill pan over medium-high heat. Add the corn and grill on all sides until slightly charred. Remove from the grill and let cool.

7   In a medium bowl, combine the serrano pepper, scallions, cilantro, lime juice, and olive oil. Cut the corn kernels off the cobs and add them to the bowl. Toss to combine and season with salt and black pepper.

8   Set up a buffet-style table with the Mexican pulled pork, peppers and onions, charred corn salad, chipotle-lime crema, avocado, queso fresco, pico de gallo, lime wedges, and flour tortillas. Invite everyone to DIY their own fajitas.

JUST THE TIPS

If you are using a traditional slow cooker instead of a multicooker, you can brown the pork and cook the peppers and onions in a sauté pan on the stovetop.

Any extra Mexican spice blend can be stored in an airtight container for up to 6 months.

FOR THE CHIPOTLE-LIME CREMA

1 cup sour cream

1 small channed chipotle pepper in adobo sauce

2 tablespoons freshly squeezed lime juice (from 1 medium lime)

1 tablespoon olive oil

1 teaspoon honey

1 cup fresh cilantro leaves

1/2 teaspoon kosher salt

FOR THE CHARRED CORN SALAD

2 ears corn, husks removed

1 serrano pepper, seeds removed, minced

2 scallions, thinly sliced

2 tablespoons finely chopped fresh cilantro

2 tablespoons freshly squeezed lime juice (from 1 medium lime)

1 tablespoon olive oil

Kosher salt and freshly ground black pepper

TO SERVE

1 avocado, sliced

Queso fresco, crumbled

Pico de gallo

1 lime, cut into wedges

Flour tortillas, warmed

Nothing but Truffle Macaroni and Cheese

PREP TIME: 20 MINUTES   **COOK TIME:** 1 HOUR
TOTAL TIME: 1 HOUR 20 MINUTES   **YIELD:** 6 TO 8 SERVINGS

No matter how intricate or fun a menu may be, if something has truffle in it, I'm ordering it. The heart knows what it wants, and if Ryan Reynolds continues to be hot and unavailable, I'll settle for the floral fungus that chefs still can't get enough of. And for the critics who say that truffle overpowers a dish, that is entirely the point, especially in a macaroni and cheese. Begone with your pessimism and bring out the truffle shaver. I'll tell you when to stop slicing, aka never.

1   Preheat the oven to 350°F. Grease a 9 x 13-inch baking dish with butter.

2   In a large nonstick skillet, melt the butter over medium-high heat until it begins to bubble. Add the bread crumbs and stir until golden brown, about 7 minutes. Remove from the heat and transfer to a medium bowl. Toss to combine with the Parmesan, parsley, and salt. Set aside.

3   Bring a large pot of salted water to a boil. Add the pasta and cook until al dente, 2 to 3 minutes less than the package instructions. Drain the pasta and let cool.

4   In a medium saucepan, melt the truffle butter over medium-high heat. Add the onion and garlic and cook until the onion is translucent and the garlic is fragrant, about 4 minutes. Gradually add the warmed milk, stirring continuously. Evenly sprinkle the flour over the top of the mixture and stir. Cook for about 2 minutes to cook out the raw taste of the flour. Bring the sauce to a boil, then reduce the heat to maintain a simmer and cook to thicken, about 7 minutes. Test the sauce to make sure it is thickened properly by running your finger through the sauce on the back of a wooden spoon. If the sauce stays separated, it is ready for you to add the cheese; if it runs together, it needs a little more time to cook. Once you are sure the sauce is properly thickened, remove it from the heat and add the fontina, cheddar, and Gruyère. Stir until the cheeses melt, then season with the nutmeg, salt, and pepper.

5   Mix in the cooked pasta. Pour into your prepared baking dish and top with the toasted bread crumb mixture. Bake for 30 minutes, until the mac and cheese is bubbling. Remove from the oven and garnish with the shaved black truffle, if using. Let cool for at least 10 minutes before serving.

4 tablespoons unsalted butter, plus more for greasing

1 cup panko bread crumbs

1/4 cup freshly grated Parmesan cheese

1/4 cup finely chopped fresh flat-leaf parsley

1 1/2 teaspoons kosher salt, plus more for seasoning

1 pound campanelle or cavatappi pasta

5 tablespoons black truffle butter

1/2 small yellow onion, finely grated

2 garlic cloves, minced

4 cups whole milk, warm

5 tablespoons all-purpose flour

4 ounces fontina cheese, grated (about 1 cup)

8 ounces sharp white cheddar cheese, grated (about 2 cups)

8 ounces Gruyère cheese, grated (about 2 cups)

1/2 teaspoon freshly ground nutmeg

Freshly ground black pepper

1 black truffle, thinly shaved, for garnish (optional)

BASIC BASICS

When making mac and cheese, you may be tempted to use truffle oil. It's easy to find and you hear people talk about it all the time. Originally, truffle oil was made using a high-quality olive oil and black or white truffles. But here's the thing: Truffle oil today is often made using synthetic truffle flavorings. That's why I have opted to use truffle butter made from fresh truffles. You can see the little flecks of truffle in the butter, making it a more gourmet and authentic experience.

Fried Chicken: A Love Story, Part II

Reaching your lowest of all lows is drunkenly ordering chicken fingers at three a.m., falling asleep, and waking up to three angry voice mails from the delivery guy the next morning. (Not that I know from personal experience or anything.) To remedy this, er, issue, it's best to make fried chicken yourself with very little judgment and a whole lot of flavor. Just look at its versatility! It can be the star of a sandwich, dipped in barbecue sauce, or even topped with marinara and mozzarella for a classic chicken Parmesan. Whatever you decide, just know that you really can't go wrong, because fried chicken is BAE, unlike that one friend who told you that perms were making a comeback and the perfect look for your precious round face.

Fried Chicken Sandwich

PREP TIME: 30 MINUTES   **COOK TIME:** 20 MINUTES
TOTAL TIME: 50 MINUTES PLUS BRINING OVERNIGHT   **YIELD:** 4 SERVINGS

1 First prepare the fried chicken: In a gallon-size zip-top bag, combine the buttermilk and hot sauce. Season the chicken with salt and pepper and add to the buttermilk. Seal the bag and marinate in the refrigerator for at least 1 hour and up to overnight.

2 Meanwhile, make the slaw: In a medium bowl, combine the napa cabbage, red cabbage, carrots, scallions, mayonnaise, vinegar, and hot sauce and season with salt and pepper. Set aside.

3 Fill a large Dutch oven with 3 inches of vegetable oil and heat the oil to 365°F. Line a baking sheet with a wire rack.

4 In a large bowl, combine the seasoned salt, garlic powder, cayenne, all-purpose flour, rice flour, cornstarch, and baking powder. Add a few tablespoons of the buttermilk mixture and mix to create clumps. This will help make the chicken extra crispy.

5 Remove the chicken from the buttermilk brine and, one piece at a time, dredge in the flour mixture. Dip back in the buttermilk and then dredge in the flour mixture again, creating a double dredge. Add the chicken to the hot oil and cook until golden brown and the internal temperature reaches 165°F, 6 to 8 minutes, flipping halfway through. Transfer to the prepared baking sheet and season with kosher salt.

6 Spread the butter evenly on the cut sides of the rolls. Heat a large skillet over medium-high heat and toast the buns until golden, about 1 minute. Transfer to a cutting board. Line the bottom of a bun with a few pickle slices. Add a piece of fried chicken and a large handful of the slaw. Sandwich with the top half of the bun and enjoy.

1 cup buttermilk

2 tablespoons hot sauce

2 (8-ounce) boneless, skinless chicken breasts, halved crosswise and pounded 1/4 inch thick

Kosher salt and freshly ground black pepper

Vegetable oil, for frying

2 teaspoons seasoned salt (like Lawry's)

1 teaspoon garlic powder

1/2 teaspoon cayenne pepper

3/4 cup all-purpose flour

3/4 cup rice flour

1/2 cup cornstarch

1 teaspoon baking powder

2 tablespoons unsalted butter, at room temperature

4 brioche buns, halved

Dill pickle slices

FOR THE SLAW

1 1/2 cups shredded napa cabbage

1/4 cup shredded red cabbage

1/4 cup shredded carrots

2 tablespoons sliced scallions

1/4 cup mayonnaise

2 tablespoons apple cider vinegar

1 teaspoon hot sauce

Kosher salt and freshly ground black pepper

JUST THE TIPS

If you have the time, brining the chicken overnight is really the way to go. It will give you the most flavor and cuts down on some of the prep.

The double dredge helps create that crispy crust that makes a piece of fried chicken amazing. Don't skimp on your dredging!

Fried Chicken Bites

PREP TIME: 20 MINUTES **COOK TIME:** 15 MINUTES
TOTAL TIME: 35 MINUTES PLUS BRINING OVERNIGHT
YIELD: 6 TO 8 SERVINGS

6 boneless, skinless chicken thighs, cut into ¹/₂-inch pieces

Kosher salt and freshly ground black pepper

1 cup dill pickle juice (from a jar of pickles)

Vegetable oil, for frying

1 cup buttermilk

1 tablespoon hot sauce

1 cup all-purpose flour

1 cup rice flour

1 tablespoon baking powder

JUST THE TIPS

This recipe is a real crowd-pleaser. Never underestimate how many fried chicken bites the group can eat. I guarantee you it's more than you think!

The special sauce from the Black Bean–Quinoa Burger on page 103 is perfect for dipping.

1 Put the chicken pieces in a gallon-size zip-top bag. Season with salt and pepper. Pour the pickle juice into the bag and seal. Marinate in the refrigerator for at least 1 hour and up to overnight.

2 Fill a medium Dutch oven with 2 inches of vegetable oil and heat the oil to 365°F. Line a baking sheet with a wire rack.

3 Drain the chicken and pat dry. In a medium bowl, combine the buttermilk and hot sauce. In another medium bowl, whisk together the all-purpose flour, rice flour, baking powder, and 1 teaspoon salt. Dip the chicken, a few pieces at a time, in the buttermilk mixture and then dredge it in the flour mixture. Transfer to a baking sheet and repeat with the remaining pieces.

4 Place the chicken, a few pieces at a time, in the hot oil and cook until golden brown and the internal temperature reads 165°F, about 5 minutes. Using a slotted spoon, transfer the chicken to the prepared baking sheet and sprinkle with salt. Repeat with the remaining chicken. Serve with your desired dipping sauce.

Chicken Parmesan

PREP TIME: 30 MINUTES   **COOK TIME:** 45 MINUTES
TOTAL TIME: 1 HOUR 15 MINUTES   **YIELD:** 4 SERVINGS

1   Preheat the oven to 400°F. Line a baking sheet with foil.

2   Season the chicken on both sides with salt and pepper. Set up your
dredging station: Put the flour in one baking dish and season with salt
and pepper; mix to combine. In a second baking dish, whisk together the
eggs and water. In a third baking dish, combine the bread crumbs and
Parmesan and season with salt and pepper.

3   One at a time, dip the seasoned chicken breasts into the flour to coat,
shaking off any excess. Then dip into the egg, followed by the bread
crumb mixture. Place temporarily on the prepared baking sheet. Repeat
with the remaining chicken breasts.

4   Heat two large oven-safe sauté pans over medium heat. Add ¼ cup of the
olive oil to each pan. Add 2 chicken breasts to each pan and cook until
golden brown on both sides, about 4 minutes. Top with the pomodoro
sauce and sliced mozzarella. Transfer the sauté pans to the oven and
bake to finish cooking the chicken and melt the cheese, about 5 minutes,
or until the internal temperature of the chicken is 165°F.

5   Remove from the oven and divide among four plates. Garnish with
additional Parmesan and basil. Serve.

4 boneless, skinless chicken
breasts (about 1½ pounds),
pounded thin

Kosher salt and freshly ground
black pepper

2 cups all-purpose flour

5 eggs, beaten

2 tablespoons water

2 cups bread crumbs

¼ cup freshly grated Parmesan
cheese, plus more for
garnish

½ cup olive oil

2 cups pomodoro sauce
(see page 121)

1 (8-ounce) ball fresh
mozzarella cheese, thinly
sliced

Fresh basil, for garnish

LITERALLY CAN'T EVEN
Chicken Parmesan can be
served on a toasted roll as a
sandwich or with pasta as a side.

Sinful Sweets

Diet who? If you're experiencing a breakup, split ends, mansplaining, or any of life's many misfortunes, these are the sweets that will get you through them all.

Or if life is going grand for you, then a) I'm jealous, share your secret; and b) these familiar indulgences are there for celebrations or to congratulate you on a job well done. Life is simply too short to not eat the damn cookie or buy one of everything at the sorority bake sale, so partake in both and counter it with spirulina, turmeric, and other fad foods in the morning. Because there's nothing more basic bitch than pretending like you don't care (#YOLO!!!) when you actually do (#FML).

4

OMG, the Best Chocolate Chip Cookies Ever!!!

PREP TIME: 5 MINUTES   **COOK TIME:** 30 MINUTES
TOTAL TIME: 35 MINUTES PLUS COOLING   **YIELD:** 6 TO 8 LARGE COOKIES

2¼ cups all-purpose flour

2 teaspoons cornstarch

1 teaspoon baking soda

¾ teaspoon coarse sea salt

¾ cup margarine

¾ cup light brown sugar

½ cup granulated sugar

1 egg

1 teaspoon vanilla extract

1½ cups milk chocolate chips

JUST THE TIPS

I opted for margarine (I use Blue Bonnet) in this recipe because it has a higher melting point than butter, making the cookies spread less and look more pillowy. If you aren't a fan of margarine, you can easily use unsalted butter in its place. Just make sure to leave more room between the cookies when baking.

Once during my former life as a publicist, an editor replied to an email from me saying, "Enough with the hyperbole!!!" to which my response was: "Get in, loser, that's my brand." I didn't actually send this reply, but I certainly thought about it, because I was truly offended. When I am excited about something, it shows. And sure, I can be a bit overdramatic at times, but not when it comes to my sister Sami's chocolate chip cookies. They're worth the over-the-top fanfare. So what's the secret? Sea salt . . . because she's fancy AF and it's a well-known culinary fact that salt enhances the flavor of practically anything you pair it with, savory or sweet. That even includes the chicken tetrazzini everyone's crazy aunt insists on bringing to every family potluck. Thank God for salt, and thank God for shameless exclamation marks!!!

1   Preheat the oven to 350°F with a rack placed in the center. Line two baking sheets with parchment paper.

2   In a small bowl, combine the flour, cornstarch, baking soda, and salt. Set aside.

3   In the bowl of a stand mixer fitted with the paddle attachment, combine the margarine, light brown sugar, and granulated sugar. Mix on medium speed until light and fluffy and fully combined. Add the egg and vanilla and mix to combine. Gradually add the flour mixture and mix on low speed until fully combined. Remove the bowl from the stand mixer and, using a rubber spatula, fold in the chocolate chips.

4   Using a ¼-cup scoop, portion the dough into 6 to 8 cookies. Place the cookies on the prepared baking sheets, making sure they are a few inches apart. Bake one sheet at a time on the center rack for about 15 minutes, until the outside is golden but the inside is still soft. Allow to cool on the baking sheet for 10 minutes before transferring to a wire rack to cool completely. Repeat with the second baking sheet.

LITERALLY CAN'T EVEN

Ghirardelli's milk chocolate chips are the only ones I ever use for this recipe. They're oversized and perfect.

Antidepressant
Red Velvet Cake Pops

PREP TIME: 1 HOUR 20 MINUTES **COOK TIME:** 40 MINUTES
TOTAL TIME: 2 HOURS PLUS CHILLING **YIELD:** ABOUT 36 CAKE POPS

You eat red velvet for the cream cheese frosting and enjoy the fact that
the bright slice, in traditional cake form, is many times the size of your face.
You don't eat red velvet to pick apart what it's actually made from, because
I really didn't know until I made these cake pops for yet another Valentine's
Day alone in bed with carbs and feelings. They say red velvet is a Southern
staple, but I happen to think it's a depression staple, along with vodka and
the overwhelming urge to slap people on the NYC subway. As a courtesy
to yourself and others, stick with the red velvet cake. It will make you much
happier, at least temporarily.

1   Preheat the oven to 350°F. Coat two 9-inch cake pans with nonstick
    spray, line the bottoms with parchment paper, then spray again.

2   First make the red velvet cake: In a large bowl, sift together the flour,
    salt, baking soda, cocoa powder, and granulated sugar. In the bowl of
    a stand mixer fitted with the paddle attachment, combine the canola oil,
    eggs, vanilla, buttermilk, vinegar, and food coloring. With the mixer on
    low speed, gradually add the dry ingredients to the wet ingredients and
    mix until they are just combined.

3   Divide the batter evenly between the prepared cake pans and bake for
    about 35 minutes. Remove from the oven and allow to cool in the pans
    for 10 minutes before flipping the cakes out onto a wire rack to cool
    completely. Discard the parchment.

4   Meanwhile, make the cream cheese frosting: In the bowl of a stand mixer
    fitted with the whisk attachment, combine the cream cheese, butter, and
    salt. Beat on medium-high speed until light and fluffy. Gradually add the
    confectioners' sugar and beat until incorporated, scraping down the sides
    of the bowl as necessary. Add the vanilla and beat to combine. Remove
    the bowl from the stand mixer.

5   Line a baking sheet with parchment paper. Trim off the edges of your
    cakes and use your hands to finely crumble the cake into a large bowl.
    Add 1 cup of the cream cheese frosting and mix to combine; let sit for
    5 minutes. Using an ice cream scoop, portion the cake mixture into
    36 balls and place on the prepared baking sheet. Chill in the refrigerator
    for about 30 minutes. This will help the balls stay together when you
    roll them.

FOR THE RED VELVET CAKE

2¹/₂ cups cake flour

1 teaspoon fine sea salt

1¹/₄ teaspoons baking soda

2 tablespoons unsweetened
   Dutch-process cocoa
   powder

1¹/₂ cups granulated sugar

1¹/₂ cups canola oil

2 eggs, at room temperature

1¹/₂ teaspoons vanilla extract

1 cup buttermilk, at room
   temperature

2 teaspoons distilled white
   vinegar

1 tablespoon red gel food
   coloring

FOR THE CREAM CHEESE FROSTING

8 ounces cream cheese,
   at room temperature

5 tablespoons unsalted butter,
   at room temperature

1 teaspoon kosher salt

1³/₄ cups confectioners' sugar

2 teaspoons vanilla extract

1 bag white Candy Melts,
   or 12 ounces white
   chocolate chips

2 tablespoons canola oil

Lollipop sticks

Red sprinkles

Styrofoam block

6   Assemble and coat your cake pops: Fill a medium saucepot with 2 inches of water and heat over medium heat. Set a large heatproof bowl on top and put the Candy Melts in the bowl. Heat, stirring, until they have melted, then add the canola oil until the coating is thinned enough for easy dipping. Stir to combine and turn off the heat.

7   Remove the balls of cake from the refrigerator and roll each tightly into a smooth ball. Dip the lollipop sticks into the coating and, one at a time, insert a lollipop stick into the center of each ball, facing up. Once all of the cake pops have lollipop sticks in them, transfer the baking sheet to the freezer to set, about 10 minutes.

8   Once set, remove from the freezer and allow to sit at room temperature for 5 minutes. (If there is too big a difference in temperature between your coating and the cake pop, it will cause the coating to crack.) One at a time, dip the cake pops in the coating. In order to keep the cake pop nice and round as the coating sets, you can either place the cake pops in a low-sided glass dish, lollipop stick facing down, or (my preference) stick the lollipop stick into a piece of styrofoam and allow to dry standing upright. Decorate your cake pops as desired; red sprinkles, if used, should be sprinkled over the cake pops before the coating sets. If using a drizzle of melted chocolate, wait for the coating to set and then drizzle with chocolate. Allow to set completely and enjoy!

JUST THE TIPS

When rolling the cake balls, make sure to really mash together the cake dough. And use a lot of force between your hands to form tight balls. They will fall apart at first, but continue to roll, roll, roll, and they will come together.

If your Candy Melts are too thick, it will be difficult to dip the cake pop into the glaze and it may fall off the lollipop stick. Make sure the coating is thin enough to dip. To be safe, you can use a spoon and pour some of the coating over the cake pop, letting the excess drip into the bowl.

Want a shortcut? You can use a boxed cake mix and/or store-bought frosting to speed up the process. Not quick enough? Doughnut holes make a great cake pop substitute.

Bedside Companion Frozen Yogurt

PREP TIME: 20 MINUTES   **TOTAL TIME:** 20 MINUTES PLUS CHILLING
YIELD: 4 CUPS

4 cups plain whole-milk yogurt, chilled

1 cup sugar

Pinch of kosher salt

JUST THE TIPS

You'll want to make sure that your yogurt is cold. Once you mix all your ingredients, chill the mixture in the refrigerator until it is about 45°F.

When ready to serve, allow the frozen yogurt to sit at room temperature for a few minutes so it is easier to scoop.

Running your ice cream scoop under hot water will also help when scooping frozen yogurt.

I can't be the only one who has an obsession with sad movies, right? It may be masochistic to sit at home and cry in bed on the weekend, but it's a good reminder that, yes, I do indeed have a soul and, yes, I do indeed probably need a therapist. It's also an excuse to nosh on healthy-ish frozen yogurt, which has always been the perfect somber food. There's something about its icy exterior that pairs well with me trying to prove that I don't share the same trait. Top it with whatever you like (for me, it's obviously peanut butter anything) and park your bowl right next to that jumbo box of tissues. It's going to be a long night.

1   Freeze the bowl of your ice cream maker for at least 24 hours.

2   In a large bowl, whisk together the yogurt, sugar, and salt. Chill the yogurt base if necessary (see "Just the Tips").

3   Pour the yogurt base into the frozen ice cream maker bowl and churn until it reaches the consistency of soft-serve ice cream, about 20 minutes. Scoop into an airtight freezer container and freeze until firm before serving, about 5 hours or overnight.

Frozen Banana "Ice Cream"

PREP TIME: 10 MINUTES PLUS CHILLING
TOTAL TIME: 10 MINUTES PLUS CHILLING   **YIELD:** ABOUT 3 CUPS

Peel the bananas and break into thirds. Place in a freezer bag and freeze for at least 5 hours but preferably overnight. Once frozen, transfer the bananas to a blender with the oat milk and peanut butter powder, if using. Blend on high speed until smooth. If you like the texture of soft-serve ice cream, feel free to enjoy this as is. If you prefer hard-serve ice cream, transfer the banana ice cream to a freezer-safe container and freeze until solid, about 5 hours. Scoop and serve.

LITERALLY CAN'T EVEN

Sometimes you're craving something cold, but just want a healthier alternative to ice cream. This is a great quick recipe to settle that craving. Feel free to experiment with the flavors. You can add cinnamon, nutmeg, coconut, or top with fresh berries.

If your bananas aren't ripe enough and you'd like your ice cream a little sweeter, add honey a tablespoon at a time until it reaches your desired sweetness.

5 ripe medium bananas

¹/₄ cup oat milk

2 tablespoons peanut butter powder (optional)

Pinch of kosher salt

THE MORE YOU GLOW

Peanut butter powder has 85 percent less fat than regular peanut butter, but is jam-packed with that flavor we love. And it's high in omega-9 fatty acids.

"I've Got My Shit Together" Strawberry Macarons

PREP TIME: 1 HOUR 45 MINUTES   **COOK TIME:** 20 MINUTES
TOTAL TIME: 2 HOURS 5 MINUTES PLUS CHILLING
YIELD: ABOUT 30 MACARONS

FOR THE MACARON SHELLS

1³/₄ cups confectioners' sugar

1 cup almond flour

¹/₄ teaspoon fine sea salt

2 tablespoons strawberry powder

3 egg whites, at room temperature

¹/₄ teaspoon cream of tartar

¹/₄ cup superfine sugar

Pink food coloring

FOR THE STRAWBERRY FILLING

1 stick unsalted butter, at room temperature

1¹/₂ cups confectioners' sugar

¹/₂ teaspoon vanilla extract

2 tablespoons strawberry puree

A girl was reading *Anna Karenina* on the train while holding a box of macarons as I was listening to Nicki Minaj's "Stupid Hoe" and swiping left repetitively on Tinder. This was a portrait of two people clearly winning at life, but in *slightly* different ways. Since basic bitches love to compare themselves with others (in an effort to be better), I went home and attempted to make macarons myself. What I found was that they were challenging (thank you, France) and temperamental (thank you, France, again), but after some trial and error, they were the perfect treat that validated the direction of my life ever so slightly. And frankly, once you turn thirty and are still living paycheck to paycheck in NYC, validation is pretty much the only thing you seek and need.

1   Line two baking sheets with silicone baking mats.

2   First make the macaron shells: In a food processor, combine the confectioners' sugar, almond flour, fine sea salt, and strawberry powder and process until smooth. Sift through a fine-mesh sieve into a large bowl. If there are any larger pieces that don't fit through the sieve, discard them.

3   In the bowl of a stand mixer fitted with the whisk attachment, beat the egg whites and cream of tartar on medium speed until light and frothy. Gradually add the superfine sugar and increase the speed. Beat until the egg whites hold shiny, stiff peaks, about 6 minutes. (You should be able to invert the bowl without the egg whites slipping out.) Add the food coloring and mix gently by hand to combine. Fold the egg whites into the almond flour mixture, making sure not to overmix. Transfer the batter to a pastry bag fitted with a ¹/₄-inch round tip.

4   Pipe 1-inch rounds of batter on the prepared baking sheets, making sure they are an inch apart. (The macaron shells will spread slightly.) Give each pan a couple of firm taps on the countertop to release air bubbles. Let sit at room temperature for 1 hour.

5   Meanwhile, make the strawberry filling: In the bowl of a stand mixer fitted with the whisk attachment, beat the butter until smooth. Gradually add the confectioners' sugar and beat until light and fluffy. Add the vanilla and strawberry puree. Beat to combine, then transfer to a piping bag fitted with a ¹/₄-inch round tip.

If you can't find strawberry powder, buy freeze-dried strawberries and process them in the food processor to a fine powder. You will need only ¼ ounce freeze-dried strawberries to make 2 tablespoons powder.

If you can't find strawberry puree, simply chop up 3 to 4 fresh strawberries and puree in a blender or food processor until smooth. To remove the seeds, strain the puree through a fine-mesh sieve.

6   Preheat the oven to 300°F, with a rack set in the middle. Bake the macaron shells, one pan at a time, on the middle rack, until they are shiny and have risen, about 16 minutes. Remove from the oven and let the pan cool completely on a wire rack. Repeat with the second pan.

7   Pipe the strawberry filling on the flat side of one of the macaron shells. Sandwich the filling layer with another macaron shell, flat-side down, creating your finished macaron. Repeat with the remaining macarons and filling. Place in a single layer in an airtight container and refrigerate overnight. Remove from the fridge and let sit at room temperature for 30 minutes before serving.

Hip, Hip, Beret: A Breakdown of Macarons

Macarons aren't exceptionally hard to make, but they do require patience and precision. They should be bite-size, have a shiny flat crust on top, a chewy interior, textured "feet," and a smooth filling between the shells.

You might be tempted to skip processing the ingredients together and sifting them, but please don't! To make a proper macaron shell, you need a smooth base.

Sure, with some other baking recipes you can fake "room temperature," but with macarons, that's a risky game. If your eggs aren't at room temperature and you don't want to wait hours, simply place them in a bowl of warm water. Egg whites that are cold do not whip up the same and will ruin your product.

Folding the egg whites into the almond flour mixture is where most people go wrong. You need to incorporate all the ingredients completely until you have a smooth, lavalike texture. You should then be able to lift up your spatula and have the batter create a figure eight. It may seem as if you have deflated your egg whites, but you want the air to distribute evenly in order to prevent the macaron shells from cracking when baking.

A common mistake is not whipping your egg whites to stiff peaks. At stiff peaks, you should be able to invert the bowl of egg whites over your head and they will remain in the bowl.

If piping isn't a skill you have mastered, you can draw circles on parchment paper as guides, allowing enough space in between to account for spreading.

Don't forget to give the baking sheets a couple of firm taps on the counter to release the air bubbles in the unbaked macaron shells before you let them sit. This helps prevent cracking while baking.

Feet: We hear people use this term, but what are they? Feet are the less smooth section of the macaron shell around the bottom edge. They form when you rest the macaron batter after piping it. Make sure to rest them for 1 hour. This helps the macaron shells bake upward and not spread outward.

Confetti Wedding, Err, Birthday Cake

PREP TIME: 1 HOUR **COOK TIME:** 45 MINUTES
TOTAL TIME: 1 HOUR 45 MINUTES **YIELD:** 8 TO 10 SERVINGS

I want a wedding. Wait, let me rephrase that. I want a wedding registry. I also want to get married just so I can customize an over-the-top cake that will surely have edible glitter, gold frosting, and a salted caramel buttercream. Until I get to this point, my birthday cake will have to suffice, and I'm completely content with busting out good ol' confetti. If vanilla cake with rainbow sprinkles doesn't induce happiness at its highest level, then I highly suggest a Xanax cake, or gently resting a birthday candle in a stiff martini and calling it a day. There's just no pleasing you.

1 Preheat the oven to 350°F. Lightly butter two 9-inch round cake pans and line the bottoms with parchment paper, then butter the parchment.

2 In a medium bowl, combine the flour, baking powder, and fine sea salt.

3 In the bowl of a stand mixer fitted with the paddle attachment, beat the butter and granulated sugar until light and fluffy, about 5 minutes. Add the eggs, one at a time, mixing well after each addition. Beat in the vanilla. Add one-third of the flour mixture, followed by half of the buttermilk. Repeat, ending with the flour. Scrape down the sides of the bowl to make sure everything is combined. Fold in the sprinkles by hand.

4 Divide the batter evenly between the prepared cake pans. Firmly tap the pans on the counter to release any air bubbles and smooth the tops with an offset spatula. Bake until the cakes are golden, pulling away from the edges of the pan, and cooked through, 35 to 40 minutes, rotating the pans halfway through. Let cool in the pans on a wire rack for 10 minutes, then turn the cakes out of the pans onto the rack and let cool completely. Discard the parchment.

5 Meanwhile, make the buttercream frosting: In the bowl of a stand mixer fitted with the whisk attachment, beat the butter on high speed until light and fluffy. Reduce the speed to low and gradually add the confectioners' sugar, beating well after each addition. Add the vanilla and salt and beat to combine. Fold in the sprinkles by hand.

6 Trim the domed tops of the cakes so they are flat and even. Discard scraps. Place one cake on a cake stand and spread an even layer of the buttercream over the top, allowing some overflow down the sides. Top with the remaining cake and repeat. Using an offset spatula or a rubber bench scraper, frost the sides of the cake, leaving some of the cake still visible. Decorate as desired with the remaining frosting and sprinkles.

FOR THE CONFETTI CAKE

2 sticks unsalted butter,
    at room temperature,
    plus more for greasing

3 cups cake flour

1 tablespoon baking powder

³/₄ teaspoon fine sea salt

2 cups granulated sugar

5 eggs

1 tablespoon vanilla extract

1¹/₂ cups buttermilk

¹/₂ cup rainbow sprinkles

FOR THE BUTTERCREAM FROSTING

3 sticks unsalted butter,
    at room temperature

3¹/₂ cups confectioners' sugar,
    sifted

³/₄ teaspoon vanilla extract

Pinch of fine sea salt

¹/₂ cup rainbow sprinkles,
    plus more for decorating

JUST THE TIPS

This recipe will make one 9-inch layer cake or 24 cupcakes. For the latter, simply reduce the baking time to 12 to 15 minutes.

Confetti cake is supposed to be fun, so go all out when decorating this cake. The crowd will love it!

Supersize S'mores with Cookie Butter

PREP TIME: 35 MINUTES **COOK TIME:** 25 MINUTES
TOTAL TIME: 1 HOUR PLUS CHILLING **YIELD:** 10 TO 12 SERVINGS

1 cup finely ground graham
    crackers (about 7 crackers)

2 cups all-purpose flour

1/2 teaspoon fine sea salt

3 sticks unsalted butter,
    at room temperature

3/4 cup sugar

1/2 cup plus 1 cup cookie butter

1 teaspoon vanilla extract

10 (1.55-ounce) rectangular
    chocolate bars

2 (10.5-ounce) bags
    large marshmallows
    (48 marshmallows total)

JUST THE TIPS

This recipe is great for
entertaining. You can assemble
your s'mores in advance and
then broil them right before
you are ready to serve. It's
bound to be a showstopper!

Let's be honest: There's nothing appealing about camping other than coming across as adventurous on social media, potentially seeing a live deer, and s'mores. But if you subject yourself to nature and its frequently horrible elements, you deserve a giant s'more elevated with cookie butter. If anything, it will serve as an excellent distraction from not having Wi-Fi or your favorite pore-clearing face mask. Traveling with someone who doesn't like cookie butter? Into the campfire they go. And now you'll have a brand-new ghost story to tell the kids when you're sitting around and eating your Supersize S'mores with Cookie Butter.

1   In a medium bowl, combine the graham cracker crumbs, flour, and salt.

2   In the bowl of a stand mixer fitted with the paddle attachment, beat the butter on medium speed until smooth. Add the sugar and beat until light and fluffy. Add ½ cup of the cookie butter and the vanilla. Add the flour mixture gradually and mix on low speed until the ingredients are fully incorporated, scraping down the sides as necessary.

3   On a lightly floured work surface, turn out the dough and divide it into two pieces. Wrap in plastic wrap and refrigerate for at least 2 hours.

4   Preheat the oven to 350°F.

5   On a piece of parchment paper cut to fit a baking sheet, roll out one piece of dough to a 14 by 10-inch rectangle, about ¼ inch thick, trimming off the excess. Repeat with the second piece of dough. Cut each rectangle in half crosswise to make two 7 by 10-inch rectangles. Transfer the dough on the parchment to two baking sheets and chill in the fridge for 10 minutes. Bake until golden brown, about 20 minutes. Remove from the oven. Score the cookies into graham crackers by creating the perforated lines for 4 rectangles on each cookie and poking with a skewer to create the small holes. Let cool completely on the baking sheets. Turn the oven to broil.

6   Line a baking sheet with parchment paper and invert one cooled cookie crust onto it. Spread evenly with ½ cup of the cookie butter. Top with 5 chocolate rectangles and place 24 marshmallows on top. Repeat with a second cookie crust and toppings. Broil for 1 to 2 minutes until the marshmallows are golden brown and the chocolate is softened. Transfer to a serving platter. Top each s'more with a second cookie crust and serve.

Honorable Peanut Butter Blondies

PREP TIME: 45 MINUTES **COOK TIME:** 30 MINUTES
TOTAL TIME: 1 HOUR 15 MINUTES PLUS CHILLING
YIELD: 9 LARGE OR 16 SMALL BLONDIES

1 stick unsalted butter, melted and cooled, plus more for greasing

1¹/₂ cups all-purpose flour

1 teaspoon baking powder

1 teaspoon fine sea salt

³/₄ cup packed light brown sugar

³/₄ cup granulated sugar

¹/₂ cup creamy peanut butter

2 eggs

2 teaspoons vanilla extract

FOR THE PEANUT BUTTER FILLING

1 cup creamy peanut butter

1 cup confectioners' sugar, sifted

FOR THE CHOCOLATE GANACHE

8 ounces semisweet chocolate chips

¹/₂ cup heavy cream

Flaky sea salt, for garnish

JUST THE TIPS

To set the blondies quicker, you can chill them in the fridge before cutting.

My favorite pan to bake brownies or blondies in is a light-colored aluminum pan. It heats up quickly in the oven and cools down quickly once you are done baking.

I know I wasn't the only gay boy who dreamed of being a Girl Scout. The nature-y, survival aspect of Boy Scouts (learning how to make a fire, use a pocketknife, kill a bear, and so on) was never really appealing, but selling baked goods in a hypercompetitive environment for prizes, all while sporting a cute vest adorned with colorful pins and patches? Sign me up. I didn't get to live out my destiny as a child, but consider these Tagalong-inspired blondies as revenge against a society that crushed my adolescent dreams. Now I can be whatever I want to be, and in this case, it's an adult who binges on Girl Scout cookie-anything whenever I'd like. On my honor.

1   Preheat the oven to 350°F. Butter the bottom and sides of a 9-inch square baking pan. Line with parchment paper and butter the parchment paper.

2   In a large bowl, whisk together the flour, baking powder, and fine sea salt.

3   In a medium bowl, whisk together the melted butter, brown sugar, granulated sugar, peanut butter, eggs, and vanilla. Gradually add the flour mixture and whisk until fully combined. Transfer to the prepared baking pan and bake for 25 to 30 minutes, until golden and set but still a little gooey in the center. Remove from the oven and let cool in the pan for 10 minutes. Remove from the pan, discard the parchment paper, and transfer to a wire rack set over a baking sheet.

4   Meanwhile, make the peanut butter filling: In a medium bowl, mix the peanut butter and confectioners' sugar until fully combined and smooth. While the blondie is still a little warm, spread the peanut butter filling over the top in an even layer using an offset spatula. If the filling is a little too firm, warm the spatula with hot water, then dry it, to help it spread more easily.

5   Make the chocolate ganache: Put the chocolate chips in a medium bowl. Set aside.

6   Heat the heavy cream in a small saucepan over medium heat until bubbles just begin to appear. Remove from the heat and pour over the chocolate chips. Let sit for 5 minutes. Stir the chocolate and cream until smooth and well combined.

7   Pour the chocolate ganache over the peanut butter layer, top with some flaky sea salt, and let sit until the ganache has set. Once set, cut the blondies into 9 large squares or 16 small squares and serve.

"This Tastes So Good, I Can't Cry" Fudge

PREP TIME: 10 MINUTES **COOK TIME:** 3 MINUTES
TOTAL TIME: 13 MINUTES PLUS CHILLING **YIELD:** 16 (2-INCH) SQUARES

I was recently on a plane with a child who cried like a Gremlin doused in acid, which led me to contemplate the one thing that might actually shut it up: food. But it couldn't be just any food, such as an animal cracker or smoothie pouch. It needed to be something so sweet, so decadent, that the child would simply have to be quiet and chew. That food was fudge. Frankly, I haven't met a fudge I didn't like. There's something about its smooth texture and headache-inducing richness that I oh-so-constantly crave. And because I associate fudge with beach-town vacations, it makes me doubly happy. This Gremlin child obviously wasn't going to think of perfecting its tan while eating it, but I can pretty much guarantee that fudge would distract it from popping ears, boredom, crying, and the multitude of other extremely rude behaviors babies feel comfortable displaying on the reg. Otherwise, it's time to resort to children's Benadryl or consider adoption programs.

1 (12-ounce) bag semisweet chocolate chips
1 (14-ounce) can sweetened condensed milk
$^1/_2$ teaspoon kosher salt
1 cup chopped walnuts, toasted (optional)
$1^1/_2$ teaspoons vanilla extract
Flaky sea salt, for garnish

LITERALLY CAN'T EVEN
Mix it up by adding different nuts, or different chocolates, or crushed candies, or even a peanut butter swirl.

1 Grease an 8-inch-square baking dish with nonstick spray and line with parchment paper. Spray the parchment paper.

2 In a large microwave-safe bowl, combine the chocolate chips, sweetened condensed milk, and salt. Microwave in 30-second intervals, stirring between each interval, for 3 minutes, until the mixture is well combined and smooth. Add the chopped walnuts, if using, and the vanilla. Pour into the prepared baking dish and smooth the top with an offset spatula. Sprinkle with flaky sea salt and refrigerate until set, about 5 hours or up to overnight. Remove from the refrigerator, cut into squares, and serve.

Beatrice's Banana Pudding

PREP TIME: 1 HOUR   **COOK TIME:** 25 MINUTES
TOTAL TIME: 1 HOUR 25 MINUTES PLUS CHILLING
YIELD: 4 (12-OUNCE) GLASSES

My friend Joe and I have named my food baby Beatrice, who tends to rear her ugly head when dishes such as banana pudding are presented to me after I *already* want to vom post–large dinner. It may seem damn near impossible to take another bite, but, like clockwork, Beatrice reminds me that I'm eating for two and I somehow make room before retreating to my apartment for a night of stretchy pants and extreme "evening" sickness, aka not-cute stomach issues. To keep Beatrice's demands at bay, banana pudding has become a staple in my diet. It's ridiculously easy to make, and quells any potential fits of rage from the monster that lives inside me. I'm also not sure when she plans to be born, so banana pudding is here to stay for the foreseeable future.

1   Preheat the oven to 450°F. Line a baking sheet with parchment paper.

2   Place the 2 halved bananas on the prepared baking sheet, skin-side down. Sprinkle with the 1 tablespoon of the granulated sugar and flip over so the skin side is up. Poke a few holes in each banana skin with a paring knife. Roast until caramelized, about 15 minutes. Remove from the oven and let cool. Discard the skins, put the caramelized bananas in a large bowl, and mash until smooth. Set aside.

3   In a medium saucepan, whisk together the remaining ⅔ cup granulated sugar, the cornstarch, and the salt. Add the milk and egg yolks and whisk until there are no lumps. Place over medium heat and bring to a boil, stirring occasionally. Reduce the heat to maintain a simmer and whisk until the mixture has thickened to the consistency of pudding, about 2 minutes. Remove from the heat, add the vanilla bean paste and butter, and stir until blended. Strain through a fine-mesh sieve into the bowl with the caramelized bananas. Stir to combine.

4   Make the whipped cream: In the bowl of a stand mixer fitted with the whisk attachment, whisk the cream, confectioners' sugar, and vanilla on medium-high speed until soft peaks form. Set aside.

5   Place a layer of 5 vanilla wafers, breaking them up if necessary, at the bottom of each of four (12-ounce) stemless wineglasses and pressed around the sides. Top with a third of the caramelized banana pudding. Next place a layer of sliced bananas on top of the pudding and pressed around the sides of the glasses. Top with another layer of pudding. Continue with one more layer of wafers, this time 6 per glass, and finish with a layer of pudding. Cover with plastic wrap and transfer to the refrigerator to chill for at least 2 hours before serving. Top with the whipped cream and decorate with additional vanilla wafers. Serve.

2 ripe large bananas, skin on, halved lengthwise, plus 3 ripe large bananas, peeled and sliced ¼ inch thick

1 tablespoon plus ⅔ cup granulated sugar

¼ cup cornstarch

½ teaspoon kosher salt

3 cups whole milk

4 egg yolks

1 teaspoon vanilla bean paste

4 tablespoons unsalted butter

1 (11-ounce) box vanilla wafers (50 total)

FOR THE WHIPPED CREAM

1 cup heavy cream

1 tablespoon confectioners' sugar

½ teaspoon vanilla extract

JUST THE TIPS

Caramelizing the bananas and adding them to the pudding enriches the banana flavor throughout.

If you would rather, you can make one large banana pudding instead of individual servings.

FOR THE CRUST

10 graham crackers

2 tablespoons sugar

1 teaspoon ground cinnamon

³/₄ teaspoon kosher salt

3 tablespoons unsalted butter, melted

1 egg white

FOR THE CUSTARD FILLING

¹/₃ cup sugar

¹/₄ cup cornstarch

³/₄ teaspoon kosher salt

1¹/₂ cups whole milk

4 egg yolks

2 tablespoons unsalted butter

1 teaspoon vanilla bean paste

1 cup plain whole-milk Greek yogurt

2 cups mixed berries (raspberries, blueberries, blackberries, baby strawberries, currants, and so on), for garnish

JUST THE TIPS

This tart could also serve as breakfast! Who's stopping you?

For a silky custard, don't forget to strain the mixture when you take it off the stovetop. You want to remove any egg that may have accidentally cooked, leaving clumps in your custard.

Fruit Tart to My Heart

PREP TIME: 15 MINUTES   **COOK TIME:** 25 MINUTES
TOTAL TIME: 40 MINUTES PLUS CHILLING   **YIELD:** 8 TO 10 SERVINGS

No, "fruit tart" isn't just what bullies called me in PE class during basketball drills. It's colorful, it's custardy, and it's probably the easiest dessert you can make, all while making you come across as a literal gourmet pastry chef. It's also the easiest dessert to customize with produce that is either in season or on your list of all-time faves. Pining for pineapple? Go for it. Lusting for lemon? Eat your heart out. Craving cantaloupe? I'm not entirely sure why (pregnant, maybe?), but you do you, girl.

1   Preheat the oven to 350°F. Coat a 9-inch tart pan with nonstick spray.

2   First make the crust: In a food processor, combine the graham crackers, sugar, cinnamon, and salt. Pulse until finely ground. Add the melted butter and egg white and pulse until the crumbs are evenly coated and the mixture holds together when pressed between your fingers. Pour the crust mixture into the prepared tart pan and, using the bottom of a measuring cup, press the dough evenly into the pan and up the sides. Bake for about 10 minutes, until the crust begins to brown. Remove from the oven and let cool completely.

3   Meanwhile, make the custard filling: In a medium saucepot, whisk together the sugar, cornstarch, and salt. Add the milk and egg yolks and whisk until smooth. Cook over medium heat, whisking occasionally, until the mixture comes to a boil. Continue to cook until it reaches a pudding-like texture, about 2 minutes. Remove from the heat and stir in the butter and vanilla bean paste until blended. Strain the pudding through a fine-mesh sieve into a bowl to remove any clumps. Cover with plastic wrap, making sure the plastic is touching the surface of the pudding to prevent a skin from forming, and let cool completely. Once cool, add the yogurt and whisk to combine. Pour into the prepared crust and smooth with an offset spatula. Chill, covered, in the refrigerator for at least 3 hours and up to 1 day before serving.

4   Arrange the berries on top of the tart. Keep chilled until ready to slice and serve.

Hot Mess Peach-Blueberry Cobbler

PREP TIME: 20 MINUTES   **COOK TIME:** 1 HOUR 15 MINUTES
TOTAL TIME: 1 HOUR 35 MINUTES   **YIELD:** 6 TO 8 SERVINGS

I once fell in love with a stripper at my best friend Katie's bachelorette party in Miami. On the outside, he was just about the prettiest thing I'd ever seen, but on the inside, he was probably just a hot mess, much like a berry cobbler. To be clear, I am definitely stereotyping here (strippers can pivot to become rocket scientists or Cardi B), and I too am a human mess who can clean up on the outside, but this is the metaphor I'm working with, so roll with it, top it with drool-worthy cornmeal drop biscuit topping, and enjoy.

FOR THE PEACH-BLUEBERRY FILLING

- 2 pounds peaches (5 to 6), peeled
- 1 teaspoon lemon zest
- 2 tablespoons freshly squeezed lemon juice (from 1 medium lemon)
- $\frac{1}{3}$ cup granulated sugar
- 2 tablespoons cornstarch
- 1 cup fresh blueberries

FOR THE CORNMEAL DROP BISCUIT TOPPING

- 1 cup all-purpose flour
- $\frac{3}{4}$ cup coarse yellow cornmeal
- $\frac{1}{4}$ cup light brown sugar
- 2 teaspoons baking powder
- 1 teaspoon kosher salt
- 6 tablespoons unsalted butter, cut into $\frac{1}{2}$-inch pieces and chilled
- $\frac{2}{3}$ cup buttermilk, plus more for brushing
- Sanding sugar, for topping

Vanilla ice cream, for serving (optional)

LITERALLY CAN'T EVEN

If peaches aren't in season when you are making this cobbler, you can use frozen peaches. Just make sure to thaw the peaches and drain their excess liquid.

1   Preheat the oven to 375°F.

2   First, make the peach-blueberry filling: Bring a medium pot of water to a boil over high heat. Fill a large bowl with ice and water, leaving a few inches of room on the top. Add the peaches to the boiling water a few at a time and cook for 30 seconds, until the skins peel off easily. Drop the peaches in the ice water to cool. Repeat with the remaining peaches. Remove from the ice bath and peel away the skins. Slice the peaches into $\frac{1}{2}$-inch-thick wedges and discard the pits. Put the wedges in a large bowl.

3   Add the lemon zest, lemon juice, granulated sugar, and cornstarch. Mix to combine. Add the blueberries and mix to combine. Pour into a 2-quart baking dish. Set aside.

4   Next make the cornmeal drop biscuit topping: In a large bowl, whisk together the flour, cornmeal, light brown sugar, baking powder, and salt. Add the butter and use your hands to incorporate it into the flour until the butter is in pea-size pieces. Add the buttermilk and stir until the batter is well combined. Using an ice cream scoop, dollop the batter on top of the peach-blueberry filling, leaving space in between the dollops, as they will expand in the oven. Brush the tops of the biscuits with buttermilk and sprinkle with sanding sugar. Bake for 1 hour to 1 hour 10 minutes, until the filling is bubbling and the biscuits are golden brown and cooked through. Tent with foil after 45 minutes if the biscuits are browning quickly. Remove from the oven and let cool for 10 minutes. Serve warm, with vanilla ice cream, if desired.

All-Amurrican Apple Pie

PREP TIME: 45 MINUTES   **COOK TIME:** 1 HOUR 5 MINUTES
TOTAL TIME: 1 HOUR 50 MINUTES PLUS CHILLING   **YIELD:** 8 TO 10 SERVINGS

Aside from football, keg parties, and seeing a woman fall off a Razor scooter last week on Fifth Avenue, there is nothing more American than apple pie. And because we all venture into the burbs' apple orchards every fall to collect social media content and bushels of apples that we have absolutely no idea what to do with, here's an all-Amurrican classic, piled high with your kindergarten teacher's fruit of choice. Don't skimp on the cinnamon, though. We could all use some extra spice in our lives. Just ask Sue Johanson (who's actually Canadian, but I digress).

1 First make the white cheddar pie dough: In a food processor, combine the flour and salt and give it a quick pulse. Add the butter and pulse until the butter reaches pea-size pieces. Slowly add the water while pulsing. Add the cheese and pulse to combine. Divide the dough in half, form each half into a disk, and wrap with plastic wrap. Chill in the refrigerator for at least 2 hours.

2 Meanwhile, make the apple filling: In a large bowl, combine the apples, light brown sugar, cinnamon, nutmeg, lemon zest, lemon juice, vanilla, and salt. Mix to combine and allow to sit for 15 minutes. Stir in the cornstarch.

3 Preheat the oven to 425°F. Grease a 9-inch pie dish with nonstick spray.

4 Roll out one dough disk on a lightly floured surface to an approximately 12-inch circle and transfer the dough to the prepared pie dish, allowing the excess to hang over the sides. Add the filling, discarding any excess juices in the bowl. Dot with the butter cubes.

5 Roll out the remaining disk of dough to a 12-inch round. Cut ten 1-inch-wide strips. To make a lattice top, lay strips of dough over the pie, leaving 1-inch gaps between each strip. Fold over alternating strips and place a new strip perpendicular to the ones on the pie. Unfold the strips and repeat, alternating the strips you fold back, until you have covered the pie and finished the lattice. Trim the excess dough from the ends of the strips hanging off the side of the pie and fold the ends of the strips under the bottom crust all around the pie. Crimp the crust.

6 Brush the dough with the egg white and sprinkle with the sanding sugar. Bake for 20 minutes. Reduce the oven temperature to 350°F and bake for another 45 minutes, tenting the pie with foil partway through if the crust is browning too quickly. Remove from the oven and allow to cool for at least 3 hours before slicing. Serve with vanilla ice cream.

FOR THE WHITE CHEDDAR PIE DOUGH

2½ cups all-purpose flour

½ teaspoon kosher salt

2 sticks unsalted butter, cut into ¼-inch pieces and chilled

6 tablespoons ice water

4 ounces extra-sharp white cheddar cheese, grated (1 cup)

FOR THE APPLE FILLING

2 pounds Granny Smith apples, peeled, cored, and sliced ¼ inch thick

2 pounds Golden Delicious apples, peeled, cored, and sliced ¼ inch thick

½ cup packed light brown sugar

½ teaspoon ground cinnamon

¼ teaspoon freshly grated nutmeg

1 teaspoon lemon zest

1 tablespoon freshly squeezed lemon juice

½ teaspoon vanilla extract

½ teaspoon kosher salt

¼ cup cornstarch

2 tablespoons unsalted butter, cubed and chilled

1 egg white, lightly beaten

1 tablespoon white sanding sugar, for sprinkling

Vanilla ice cream, for serving

JUST THE TIPS

White cheddar in the crust might sound strange to you, but the combination of cheddar cheese and apple gives this pie an unexpected pop. Even noncrust lovers will scarf this down!

Leftover pie can be stored at room temperature for up to 3 days.

Single AF Cheesecake, aka the Cheesecake that Stands Alone

PREP TIME: 50 MINUTES   **COOK TIME:** 2 HOURS
TOTAL TIME: 2 HOURS 50 MINUTES PLUS CHILLING OVERNIGHT
YIELD: 8 TO 10 SERVINGS

When I had my first SJP sighting, I felt it was God's way of saying, "You can now leave New York." And while I'm tempted to move every single day of my life because of the subway, constant garbage smell, and influx of tourists who stroll way too casually on the sidewalk, I would certainly miss the cheesecake. Cheesecake is supreme, especially this sexy version topped with chocolate-covered strawberries, because one dessert, like one man, is never fulfilling. This is also another fab option for Valentine's Day if you've decided to write men off forever and replace them with empty calories and that creepy one-armed boyfriend pillow that keeps popping up in my Facebook ads. (They know me so well.)

FOR THE CRUST

1 stick unsalted butter, melted

1^1/$_2$ cups graham cracker crumbs (10 crackers)

1 tablespoon sugar

^{1}/$_2$ teaspoon kosher salt

FOR THE FILLING

1^1/$_2$ pounds cream cheese, at room temperature

1^1/$_4$ cups sugar

^{1}/$_2$ teaspoon kosher salt

1 cup sour cream, at room temperature

6 eggs, at room temperature

2 teaspoons vanilla extract

^{1}/$_2$ teaspoon finely grated lemon zest

FOR THE CHOCOLATE-COVERED STRAWBERRIES

8 ounces semisweet chocolate, chopped

4 ounces white chocolate, chopped

Canola oil

1 pound strawberries with stems

1   First make the crust: Preheat the oven to 325°F. Brush a 9-inch springform pan with some of the melted butter.

2   Put the remaining butter in a large bowl and toss with the graham cracker crumbs, sugar, and salt. Press the graham cracker mixture into the springform pan in an even layer. Bake until golden brown, about 15 minutes. Remove from the oven and let cool completely. Wrap the bottom and sides of the pan with foil and place in a roasting pan. Set aside.

3   Meanwhile, make the filling: In the bowl of a stand mixer fitted with the paddle attachment, combine the cream cheese, sugar, and salt and beat until light and fluffy. Add the sour cream and the eggs, one at a time, beating well after each addition. Add the vanilla and lemon zest and mix until just incorporated. Pour the filling into the prepared crust.

4   Transfer the roasting pan to the oven and pour boiling water into the roasting pan so that it comes about halfway up the side of the springform pan. Bake for 1 hour to 1 hour 10 minutes, until the cheesecake is set but the center still has a jiggle to it. Turn off the oven and crack open the oven door. Leave the cheesecake inside, allowing the residual heat of the oven to finish cooking the cake, about 30 minutes. Remove the cheesecake from the oven and let cool to room temperature, about 3 hours. Wrap the cheesecake in plastic and chill in the refrigerator overnight.

5　Make the chocolate-covered strawberries: Line a baking sheet with parchment paper.

6　Place the semisweet chocolate and white chocolate in two separate medium glass bowls. Heat two medium saucepots with 2 inches of water over medium heat and place the glass bowls over the pots. Heat, stirring occasionally, until all the chocolate has melted. If you find the chocolate is a little thick, you can drizzle in 1 tablespoon of canola oil at a time, mixing well after each addition, to loosen it. Turn off the heat but leave the bowls over the saucepots.

7　Pat dry the strawberries and, one at a time, dip the strawberries in the semisweet chocolate and place them on the prepared baking sheet. Dip a fork in the white chocolate and drizzle it over the chocolate-covered strawberries. Put aside until the chocolate is set, about 1 hour.

8　Remove the cheesecake from the refrigerator and take off the springform ring. Transfer to a serving plate. Garnish with the chocolate-covered strawberries. Slice and serve.

JUST THE TIPS
Store your cheesecake in the refrigerator, covered in plastic wrap, for up to 5 days.

LITERALLY CAN'T EVEN
Feel free to switch up the crust. You can use chocolate wafer cookies, vanilla wafer cookies, or gingersnap cookies—just make sure you have 1$\frac{1}{2}$ cups of crumbs.

Flourless Chocolate-Nutella Mug Cake: It's a Lifestyle

PREP TIME: 5 MINUTES   **COOK TIME:** 2 MINUTES
TOTAL TIME: 7 MINUTES   **YIELD:** 1 MUG

¼ cup Nutella (or any other good quality chocolate-hazelnut spread)

1 egg

1 tablespoon maple syrup

1 teaspoon unsweetened Dutch-process cocoa powder

1 teaspoon vanilla extract

Pinch of kosher salt

Confectioners' sugar, for dusting

JUST THE TIPS

For a fudgier cake, simply microwave for less time.

Summer is when our body goals magically align with our dessert preferences: light as a feather. And nothing is lighter and more satisfying than a flourless chocolate mug cake. This is for the gal who needs a sweet indulgence and needs it fast. She doesn't have time to slave in the kitchen and bake an entire cake, nor does she go against the Bible's advice to "lead us not into temptation" by eating beyond a single serving. She's also a huge fan of Nutella—like everyone on earth—so she finds a way to sneak it in and feels really good about it. Aim high and be the Flourless Chocolate-Nutella Mug Cake girl. You won't regret it.

In a small bowl, whisk together the Nutella, egg, maple syrup, cocoa powder, vanilla, and salt. Pour into a large (about 12-ounce) microwave-safe mug. Microwave for 1 minute to 1 minute 30 seconds. The cake will expand in the microwave and come up over the top of the mug. Let cool for 5 minutes before eating. Dust with confectioners' sugar and enjoy straight out of the mug!

Satisfyingly Simple
Strawberry Shortcake

PREP TIME: 35 MINUTES   **COOK TIME:** 25 MINUTES
TOTAL TIME: 1 HOUR   **YIELD:** 8 TO 10 SERVINGS

4 cups fresh strawberries, hulled and quartered

1 tablespoon lemon zest

2 tablespoons freshly squeezed lemon juice (from 1 medium lemon)

1/2 cup plus 2 tablespoons granulated sugar

2 1/2 cups all-purpose flour

2 teaspoons baking powder

1/2 teaspoon baking soda

1 teaspoon kosher salt

10 tablespoons (1 1/4 sticks) unsalted butter, cut into small pieces and chilled, plus 3 tablespoons unsalted butter, melted

1 1/4 cups buttermilk

2 tablespoons raw sugar

FOR THE WHIPPED CREAM

2 cups heavy cream

2 tablespoons confectioners' sugar

1/2 teaspoon vanilla extract

JUST THE TIPS

You can make the biscuits and macerate the strawberries in advance. When ready to serve, whip the cream and build the shortcakes.

Biscuits can be made 3 days in advance and stored in an airtight container at room temperature or frozen for up to 3 months.

Don't have buttermilk? Stir together 2 1/2 teaspoons lemon juice and 1 1/4 cups milk and let it sit for a couple of minutes. Then it's ready to use!

For those who think strawberry shortcake is too simple a dessert: I don't want to hear it, much like when I wear my headphones in the office while not actually listening to music. It may consist of only a few ingredients, but they're damn good ingredients that create a summertime treat that is worthy of a suspiciously happy cartoon character bearing the same name. My only gripe is when chefs and amateur cooks skimp on the whipped cream. If I'm allowing you to put fruit in a dessert with cake, you better mask that atrocity real quick or we're going to have some serious problems. Please and thank you.

1   Preheat the oven to 450°F. Line a baking sheet with parchment paper.

2   In a medium bowl, toss the strawberries, lemon zest, lemon juice, and 1/2 cup of the granulated sugar. Cover with plastic wrap and refrigerate while preparing the biscuits.

3   In a large bowl, whisk together the flour, baking powder, baking soda, salt, and remaining 2 tablespoons granulated sugar. Using a pastry blender or your hands, work the cold butter into the flour mixture, breaking it up into pea-size pieces. Add the buttermilk and knead until the dough just comes together.

4   Turn the dough out onto a lightly floured surface and press it into a 1 1/2-inch-thick round. Using a 2 1/2-inch biscuit cutter (or an upside-down glass about the same size), cut the dough into biscuits and transfer to the prepared baking sheet, placing the rounds 2 inches apart. Gather the scraps of dough and press them into a 1 1/2-inch-thick round. Cut more biscuits and transfer to the prepared baking sheet. Discard any remaining scraps. Brush the biscuits with the melted butter and sprinkle with the raw sugar.

5   Bake the biscuits until golden brown, 20 to 25 minutes. Remove from the oven and cool on a wire rack.

6   Meanwhile, make the whipped cream: In the bowl of a stand mixer fitted with the whisk attachment, combine the cream, confectioners' sugar, and vanilla. Whisk on medium-high speed until soft peaks form. Set aside.

7   Slice the biscuits in half horizontally and place the bottom halves on a platter or plate. Add the strawberries and a dollop of whipped cream. Top with the biscuit tops.

Immortalized Unicorn Cupcakes

PREP TIME: 1 HOUR 15 MINUTES   **COOK TIME:** 15 MINUTES
TOTAL TIME: 1 HOUR 30 MINUTES PLUS COOLING   **YIELD:** 24 CUPCAKES

Just when you thought the unicorn craze died like the Magnificent Seven's bangs and R. Kelly's reputation, I'm here to tell you that the mythical creature lives on forever. Sure, the average unicorn may not appreciate the fact that it's been memorialized in the form of glittery pastels and icing, but wouldn't you prefer that over a broken tombstone in an overcrowded cemetery? I sure would (unless that tombstone was made of Carrara marble or something super pretty and expensive). As long as the horn is present, I guess that's all that really matters. People appreciate horniness, whether we like to admit it or not.

1 First make the unicorn horn: Tear off two equal-size small balls of the white molding chocolate. One at a time, roll each ball between your hands to create a cone shape. Place the cones on top of each other, facing the same direction. Pick up the cones and, using your two fingers, gently twist the molding chocolate from the small tapered end down, until you have a horn shape that is roughly 1½ inches long. Trim the excess molding chocolate off the bottom. Stick a toothpick into the bottom of the horn and set the horn on a plate or small tray. Repeat until you have 24 horns. Refrigerate at least 30 minutes to harden them up a bit.

2 Put ¼ teaspoon of gold luster dust in a small shallow bowl. Dip a small brush into a bit of vodka (you need only a very small amount) and mix it with the gold luster dust to create a paste. (The vodka evaporates, it just allows the gold luster to adhere to the molding chocolate better. You could use water instead, although it is less effective.) Gently brush the horns with the golden paste to coat completely. Set aside to dry for 10 minutes.

3 Make the cupcakes: Preheat the oven to 350°F. Line two standard muffin tins with cupcake liners.

4 In a medium bowl, combine the cake flour, baking powder, and sea salt. Set aside.

5 In the bowl of a stand mixer fitted with the paddle attachment, beat the butter and granulated sugar until light and fluffy, about 5 minutes. Add the eggs, one at a time, making sure to mix well after each addition. Mix in the vanilla. Add one-third of the flour mixture, followed by half of the buttermilk. Repeat, then add the remaining flour mixture. Scrape down the sides of the bowl to make sure everything is combined.

FOR THE UNICORN HORN
White molding chocolate
Gold luster dust
Vodka

FOR THE CUPCAKES
3 cups cake flour
1 tablespoon baking powder
³/₄ teaspoon fine sea salt
2 sticks unsalted butter, at room temperature, plus more for greasing
2 cups granulated sugar
5 eggs
1 tablespoon vanilla extract
1¹/₂ cups buttermilk
Neon-pink food coloring
Neon-purple food coloring

FOR THE FROSTING
3 sticks unsalted butter, at room temperature
3¹/₂ cups confectioners' sugar, sifted
³/₄ teaspoon vanilla extract
Pinch of fine sea salt
Neon-pink food coloring
Neon-blue food coloring
Neon-yellow food coloring

6   Pour half of the batter into a separate bowl, add a few drops of pink food coloring, and mix until you have a neon-pink color. Add a few drops of purple food coloring to the batter remaining in the mixer bowl, and mix until you have a neon-purple color.

7   Using two 1-ounce scoops, at the same time drop one scoop of purple and one scoop of pink into one of the cupcake liners so that you have a half-pink, half-purple cupcake. Repeat with remaining batter until all the liners are full. Bake for 12 to 15 minutes, until the top of the cupcake springs back when you press it lightly. Remove from the oven and let cool completely.

8   Meanwhile, make the frosting: In the bowl of a stand mixer fitted with the paddle attachment, beat the butter on high speed until light and fluffy. Reduce the speed to low and gradually add the confectioners' sugar, beating until well combined. Add the vanilla and salt and beat to combine.

9   Divide the frosting evenly among three bowls. Add a few drops of pink food coloring to one bowl and mix until you have a neon-pink color. Add a few drops of blue food coloring to another bowl and mix until you have a neon-blue color. Add a few drops of yellow food coloring to the remaining bowl and mix until you have a neon-yellow color.

10 Transfer each of the frosting colors to its own disposable piping bag. Cut off the tip of each, then place all three bags in a large piping bag fitted with a large star tip. (This will swirl the frosting color as you are piping.) Pipe the frosting onto the cooled cupcakes. Top each with a unicorn horn and serve.

JUST THE TIPS

If you love the idea of unicorn cupcakes but need a shortcut, feel free to use a boxed white cake mix to make the cupcakes. They won't be as delicious, but they will still look beautiful!

Picture-Perfect Pumpkin Pie

PREP TIME: 1 HOUR   **COOK TIME:** 2 HOURS 20 MINUTES
TOTAL TIME: 3 HOURS 20 MINUTES   **YIELD:** 1 PIE (8 SERVINGS)

FOR THE PIE CRUST

2 cups all-purpose flour

1 1/2 teaspoons salt

1 teaspoon sugar

1 stick unsalted butter, cut into
1/2-inch pieces and chilled

6 to 7 tablespoons ice water

FOR THE PUMPKIN FILLING

1 (2-pound) sugar pumpkin,
halved, seeds removed

1 tablespoon olive oil

3 eggs

1/2 cup heavy cream

1/2 cup maple syrup

1 teaspoon ground cinnamon

1/2 teaspoon ground ginger

1/4 teaspoon freshly grated
nutmeg

1 teaspoon kosher salt

Whipped cream (see page 155),
for serving

JUST THE TIPS

Don't have time to roast off
your own pumpkin? You can
always use store-bought
pumpkin puree. Just make
sure it is pure pumpkin without
any additional flavorings.

To amp up the fall feel, use
a small leaf-shaped cookie
cutter to cut out little leaves
with the scraps of your dough.
Add the leaves to the crust,
pressing to adhere, and bake
for a fall-decorated pie!

There is a depressing episode of *Full House* where they are trying to honor
their dead mom during Thanksgiving by cooking family traditions. Stephanie
drops the "Picture-Perfect Pumpkin Pie" and ruins everything, as she always
does. Now, every Thanksgiving, it's become a Skladany tradition for my sister
and me to call the pumpkin pie "picture perfect" and pretend we're about to
drop it. This either makes us clever and hilarious or utterly insensitive (likely
the latter). Regardless, you'll want to *not* drop this Picture-Perfect Pumpkin
Pie, sweetened with maple syrup, which absolutely deserves a spot on this
year's holiday dinner table. Or, if you're anything like my dad, a spot under
a mountain of whipped cream that rivals the height of Kilimanjaro.

1　First make the piecrust: In a food processor, combine the flour, salt,
and sugar. Pulse to combine. Add the butter and pulse until the butter
is broken down into pea-size pieces. Slowly drizzle in the water while
pulsing until the dough just comes together. On a clean work surface,
gather the dough together and form it into a disk. Wrap the dough in
plastic wrap and refrigerate for at least 30 minutes.

2　Preheat the oven to 375°F.

3　Place the dough on a lightly floured work surface and roll it out into a
14-inch round. Transfer the dough to a 9-inch deep-dish pie plate, allowing
the excess dough to hang off the edges. Trim the overhanging dough to
1 inch. Fold the dough under itself and crimp the edges. Chill in the fridge
for 15 minutes. Line the dough with parchment paper and fill with pie
weights or dried beans. Bake for 20 minutes. Remove the parchment and
the weights or beans and bake for 15 minutes longer, until golden in color.
Remove the crust from the oven and let cool completely before adding the
filling. Raise the oven temperature to 400°F.

4　Make the pumpkin filling: Line a baking sheet with foil.

5　Drizzle the pumpkin with the olive oil and then place it cut-side down
on the prepared baking sheet. Bake until tender, 35 minutes. Let cool.
Reduce the oven temperature to 350°F.

6　Scoop the flesh of the pumpkin into a food processor (You should have
about 2 cups). Add the eggs, cream, maple syrup, cinnamon, ginger,
nutmeg, and salt. Pulse to combine. Pour the filling into the cooled pie
crust and smooth the top. Bake until the center is firm, 60 to 70 minutes.
Let cool completely. Serve with whipped cream.

Let's Chalk It Up to Chocolate Bars

PREP TIME: 40 MINUTES   **COOK TIME:** 25 MINUTES
TOTAL TIME: 1 HOUR 5 MINUTES PLUS COOLING   **YIELD:** 16 BARS

An annual reminder for those who invite me to haunted houses: Don't. But I'm always down to consume colossal amounts of Halloween chocolate, especially if it's coated or filled with nuts, seeds, dried fruit, or even quinoa. Dark chocolate provides antioxidants. And you know what else it provides? A vessel for peppermint to make bark. As someone who is essentially a self-described elf from the North Pole, this is always a welcome and refreshing topping to accompany Mariah's "All I Want for Christmas Is You." Except all I really want for Christmas is definitely more peppermint bark.

1   For the crispy quinoa: Preheat the oven to 350°F. Line an 8-inch-square baking dish with parchment paper. Grease a baking sheet with nonstick spray.

2   Toss the cooked quinoa with the coconut oil and spread it evenly over the prepared baking sheet. Bake for 20 to 25 minutes, stirring halfway through, until golden and crispy. Remove from the oven and let cool completely.

3   In a food processor, combine the dates, walnuts, cashews, pumpkin seeds, and coconut flakes. Process until finely ground. Add the cacao nibs, cashew butter, hemp seeds, wheat germ, and goji berries and process until combined. Add the crispy quinoa and pulse to mix.

4   Press the date mixture over the bottom of the prepared baking dish in an even layer, using the bottom of a measuring cup to press it down firmly. Pour the melted chocolate over the top and spread it into an even layer. Sprinkle with flaky sea salt. Transfer the baking dish to the refrigerator to chill for at least 4 hours. Remove from the fridge and cut into 16 bars. Store in an airtight container, separated by waxed paper, in the freezer for up to 3 months.

LITERALLY CAN'T EVEN

It's important to use Medjool dates for this recipe. They are softer in texture, so they break up easily and have a rich, caramel-like taste.

Feel free to switch up the garnish. Use broken-up peppermint sticks for the holidays. Decorate with sprinkles or add crushed-up candies.

³/₄ cup cooked quinoa

1 tablespoon coconut oil

1¹/₂ cups Medjool dates (about 9 ounces), pitted

¹/₂ cup walnuts

¹/₄ cup roasted salted cashews

¹/₄ cup hulled pumpkin seeds

¹/₄ cup sweetened coconut flakes

¹/₄ cup cacao nibs

¹/₂ cup cashew butter

2 tablespoons hulled hemp seeds

2 tablespoons wheat germ

¹/₄ cup goji berries

8 ounces dark chocolate, melted

Flaky sea salt, for topping

THE MORE YOU GLOW

Cacao nibs are naturally low in sugar and are a good source of fiber, protein, and healthy fats.

Yes, hemp seeds are from the same species as cannabis (marijuana), but they have many health properties. They are rich in healthy fats, protein, and minerals, but contain only trace amounts of THC (you won't get high). The flavor is mildly nutty.

Wheat germ is part of the wheat kernel and a good source of vegetable protein, fiber, and healthy fats. It's also high in vitamin E.

Goji berries contain all nine essential amino acids. They are high in fiber, iron, vitamin A, zinc, vitamin C, and antioxidants.

Hallucinatory Hot Fudge and Salted Caramel Sundae

PREP TIME: 15 MINUTES **COOK TIME:** 20 MINUTES
TOTAL TIME: 35 MINUTES **YIELD:** 4 SERVINGS

Overly optimistic people really freak me out, but finding myself in the mere presence of salted caramel can have me believing that the earth is flat and global warming is a hoax invented by the Chinese. Mix that with hot fudge and dump it on ice cream, and you'll have me believing that I should change my career to motivational speaker—a far departure from my typical request for a giant meteor to hit planet Earth. Moral of the story: Salted caramel has the power to make you believe there is literally nothing wrong in the world. If only it didn't have the calories.

1   First make the salted caramel sauce: In a heavy-bottomed medium saucepan, heat the sugar and water over medium heat until the sugar dissolves. Do not stir, but instead swirl the pan. Increase the heat and bring the sugar syrup to a boil, continuing to swirl the pan. Use a wet pastry brush to wipe down any sugar crystals forming on the sides of the pan. Boil until deep amber in color, 5 to 6 minutes. Remove from the heat and whisk in the cream. The mixture will bubble vigorously. Stir in the butter cubes and salt. Allow the caramel sauce to cool, then pour into a mason jar.

2   Next make the hot fudge sauce: Set a medium heatproof bowl over a medium saucepan filled with a couple of inches of water. Heat until the water is simmering. In the bowl, combine the bittersweet chocolate, cream, corn syrup, sugar, coffee, vanilla, and salt. Heat, stirring, until the chocolate melts and the sauce comes together, 8 minutes. Remove from the heat and let cool, then pour into a mason jar.

3   Make the sundaes: Divide the gelato evenly among four bowls. Drizzle with salted caramel sauce and hot fudge sauce. Sprinkle with the chopped walnuts. Top with a dollop of whipped cream and a maraschino cherry. Enjoy!

FOR THE SALTED CARAMEL SAUCE

1 cup sugar

1/4 cup water

3/4 cup heavy cream

6 tablespoons unsalted butter, cubed

1 teaspoon kosher salt

FOR THE HOT FUDGE SAUCE

8 ounces bittersweet chocolate, finely chopped

1 cup heavy cream

2 tablespoons light corn syrup

2 tablespoons sugar

1 teaspoon instant coffee granules

1 teaspoon vanilla extract

1/2 teaspoon kosher salt

FOR THE SUNDAES

1 pint vanilla bean gelato

1 pint salted caramel gelato

1/2 cup walnuts or roasted, salted peanuts, chopped for garnish

Whipped cream (see page 155), for garnish

Maraschino cherries, for garnish

JUST THE TIPS

The salted caramel and hot fudge sauces will keep in their jars in the refrigerator for up to 2 weeks.

Supz Sour Watermelon Gummy Bears

PREP TIME: 20 MINUTES **COOK TIME:** 10 MINUTES
TOTAL TIME: 30 MINUTES PLUS CHILLING
YIELD: ABOUT 76 GUMMY BEARS

¹/₃ cup water

3 tablespoons unflavored powdered gelatin (from one 1-ounce box)

1 cup fresh watermelon juice

¹/₃ cup plus ³/₄ cup sugar

Red food coloring (optional)

2 teaspoons citric acid

JUST THE TIPS

You will need to purchase gummy bear molds for this recipe. Use the 1-inch mold that comes with 38 gummy bear slots.

After coating the bears, you can store them at room temperature in an airtight container to keep them from becoming slimy.

So my new thing is bingeing on candy at three p.m., which leads to my not new thing of complaining about how fat I feel. My candy of choice? Sour varieties, of course. I love anything that makes my eyes water and mouth pucker, which sounds like a personal problem but is something I've enjoyed since fifth grade, when I literally sold Warheads to less intelligent classmates. (Black cherry would go for $2 a pop!) Scam artist? Nah. Visionary entrepreneur? Heck, yes. My business was so lucrative that they ultimately banned Warheads from our playground. And while I haven't perfected a Warheads imitation, these sour gummy bears are equal parts satisfying and darling, making them a basic bitch snack-time staple that I'd absolutely sell for $2 a bear ($4 if they're made with vodka).

1 Put the water in a small bowl. Sprinkle the gelatin over the water and let sit for 5 minutes.

2 In a small saucepan over medium heat, combine the watermelon juice and ⅓ cup of the sugar. Bring to a simmer and stir until the sugar has dissolved. Add the gelatin mixture and whisk until dissolved. Add a few drops of red food coloring, if using, and whisk to combine. Remove from the heat and pour into two 1-inch gummy bear molds. Refrigerate until set, about 20 minutes.

3 Unmold the gummy bears onto a baking sheet lined with parchment paper. Let the bears sit at room temperature, uncovered, for 24 hours to dry. They will shrink slightly and become chewy.

4 In a large bowl, combine the remaining ¾ cup sugar and the citric acid. Add the gummy bears and toss to coat. Enjoy.

LITERALLY CAN'T EVEN

Not a fan of watermelon? You can substitute any flavor juice you'd like.

Booze it up by soaking these overnight in rum (Rummy Bears) or vodka as an adult treat. They won't taste as good, but they'll get you tipsy.

Tira-my-su

PREP TIME: 30 MINUTES **TOTAL TIME:** 30 MINUTES PLUS CHILLING
YIELD: 8 TO 10 SERVINGS

My tea cabinet is one Metamucil and cat furball away from me being a certified grandma. But tea doesn't have to be reserved for the sick, royal, or elderly. In fact, I always prefer tea over coffee, unless it's used as an ingredient in desserts. There's just no hating tiramisu, perhaps coffee's best example of how it can shine when presented with lots of sugar and lots of cream. Be sure to really soak those ladyfingers, though, and turn them into lady rows of mushy deliciousness. Nobody likes a dry base, unless you're a cheerleader who's about to be thrown in the air, in which case you better hope the person beneath you is sober, able, and not relying on divine intervention to catch your clumsy ass.

1 In the bowl of a stand mixer fitted with the whisk attachment, whisk together the egg yolks and sugar until pale yellow in color and doubled in size, and a light ribbon forms when you lift the whisk out of the bowl, about 5 minutes. Transfer to a large bowl and set aside.

2 Wipe out the bowl of the stand mixer and add the cream. Whip until soft peaks form. Slowly add the mascarpone and whip until medium peaks form. Remove the bowl from the stand mixer and fold the egg yolk mixture into the mascarpone mixture until combined.

3 In a shallow bowl, whisk together the espresso and liqueur to combine and set aside.

4 Using a fine-mesh sieve, sprinkle the bottom of a 8-inch-square baking dish with 1 tablespoon of the cocoa powder.

5 One at a time, dip the ladyfingers into the espresso mixture and arrange them over the bottom of the baking dish in one even layer. If there are gaps, break up the ladyfingers to fill them. Spread half the mascarpone mixture over the ladyfingers. Repeat with the remaining ladyfingers and top with the remaining mascarpone mixture. Cover with plastic wrap and let sit in the refrigerator for at least 3 hours or up to overnight before serving. Sprinkle the top with the remaining 1 tablespoon cocoa powder and garnish with chocolate shavings. Enjoy.

LITERALLY CAN'T EVEN
If you can't find tiramisu liqueur, feel free to use cognac, Marsala, amaretto, or brandy.

6 egg yolks

³/₄ cup sugar

¹/₂ cup heavy cream

3 (8-ounce) containers mascarpone cheese, at room temperature

1¹/₂ cups espresso

³/₄ cup tiramisu liqueur (or cognac)

2 tablespoons unsweetened Dutch-process cocoa powder

28 to 30 Italian ladyfingers

2 ounces bittersweet chocolate, for shaving

JUST THE TIPS

For this recipe, the eggs are not cooked. Try to buy pasteurized eggs at the grocery store. They are safe to consume raw.

There are soft ladyfingers and there are hard ladyfingers. If you're using the soft ladyfingers, brush them with the espresso mixture rather than dipping them. This will keep them from falling apart. The hard ladyfingers can stand up to a quick dip.

Bow-Wow Peanut Butter–Hazelnut Puppy Chow

PREP TIME: 20 MINUTES   **COOK TIME:** 5 MINUTES
TOTAL TIME: 25 MINUTES PLUS SETTING   **YIELD:** 13 CUPS

Woof. This is a really dangerous snack to make if you participate in certain late-night weekend "recreational" activities. But if you do find yourself in that position, may God have mercy on your stomach, because you'll easily house this childhood treat in less than the amount of time it takes to prepare it. Wine pairings with desserts are now all the rage, but I recommend pairing this one with a nice antacid. The chalkiness of the calcium carbonate really strikes a lovely balance with the pepsin of your reflux and will surely prevent any aversion to making and enjoying another addictive bowl again.

FOR THE PEANUT BUTTER PUPPY CHOW

4 cups Rice Chex cereal

³/₄ cup semisweet chocolate chips

¹/₂ cup peanut butter

³/₄ teaspoon kosher salt

³/₄ cup confectioners' sugar

1 cup peanut M&M's

FOR THE HAZELNUT PUPPY CHOW

4 cups Rice Chex cereal

³/₄ cup semisweet chocolate chips

³/₄ cup hazelnut spread

³/₄ teaspoon kosher salt

³/₄ cup confectioners' sugar

1   Line two baking sheets with parchment paper.

2   For the peanut butter puppy chow: Put the cereal in a large glass bowl. In a microwave-safe bowl, microwave the chocolate chips and peanut butter on high in 30-second intervals, stirring after each until combined, about 2 minutes. Stir in the salt. Add to the bowl of cereal and, using a rubber spatula, toss to coat. Pour into a zip-top bag and add the confectioners' sugar. Toss to combine. Add the peanut M&M's and give it another toss. Pour onto one of the prepared baking sheets and spread into an even layer. Let sit until the chocolate is set, 30 minutes.

3   For the hazelnut puppy chow: Put the cereal in a large glass bowl. In a microwave-safe bowl, microwave the chocolate chips and hazelnut spread on high in 30-second intervals, stirring until warmed, about 2 minutes. Stir in the salt. Add to the bowl of cereal and, using a rubber spatula, toss to coat. Pour into a zip-top bag and add the confectioners' sugar. Toss to combine. Pour onto the second prepared baking sheet and spread into an even layer. Let sit until the chocolate is set, 30 minutes.

4   Toss both puppy chow varieties in a large bowl and serve.

Almost-Too-Pretty-to-Eat Sugar Cookies

PREP TIME: 30 MINUTES   **COOK TIME:** 20 MINUTES PLUS CHILLING
TOTAL TIME: 50 MINUTES PLUS CHILLING
YIELD: ABOUT 40 (2¹/₂-INCH) ROUND COOKIES

Parsley aside, I can go through the holidays without eating a single vegetable. Instead, my diet consists mostly of sugar cookies, sometimes in the shapes of vegetables like Christmas trees (a reach, I know) and holly (an even bigger reach), but definitely nothing green. Except green frosting. Okay, so maybe I've actually found a way to say I eat my greens and vegetables during the holidays? Now that you've got a feel for how my brain operates, you can a) pity what my parents went through during dinnertime when I was a child; and b) justify your excessive sugar cookie consumption with this tried-and-true brown-butter recipe that is scrumptious year-round. Just be ready to embrace your inevitable spot on the naughty list, which, honestly, is the more fun place to be.

2 sticks unsalted butter
1 cup granulated sugar
1 egg, at room temperature
1 teaspoon vanilla extract
2¹/₂ cups all-purpose flour
2 teaspoons baking powder
¹/₂ teaspoon fine sea salt

FOR THE ROYAL ICING
2 cups confectioners' sugar
3 to 4 tablespoons whole milk
1 tablespoon light corn syrup
Food coloring

Sprinkles (optional)
Glitter (optional)
Sanding sugar (optional)

1   Preheat the oven to 350°F. Line two baking sheets with silicone baking mats.

2   In a small saucepan over medium heat, melt the butter, swirling the pan, until golden brown in color, about 10 minutes. The butter should smell nutty. Pour the brown butter into a bowl to stop the cooking process. Chill in the refrigerator for 1 hour.

3   In the bowl of a stand mixer fitted with the paddle attachment, cream the butter and sugar. Add the egg and vanilla and beat well.

4   In a medium bowl, mix the flour, baking powder, and salt. With the mixer on low speed, slowly add the flour mixture to the butter mixture until fully incorporated.

5   On a lightly floured surface, roll the cookie dough out into a ¹/₄-inch-thick round. Using a 2¹/₂-inch round cookie cutter, cut the cookies out and place on the prepared baking sheets. Bake for 7 to 10 minutes. Remove from the oven and let cool completely.

6   Meanwhile, make the royal icing: In a medium bowl, whisk together the confectioners' sugar and milk until smooth. Add the corn syrup and whisk until the icing is smooth and glossy. Divide the icing into bowls and add as many food colorings as you'd like. Whisk to combine.

7   Dip the cooled cookies in the royal icing, spread it on with a small offset spatula or knife, or pipe it onto the cookies. Feel free to use a toothpick to draw designs. Top with sprinkles, glitter, or sanding sugar, if desired.

Brunch

The Most Important Meal of the Day

Replace Hermione's famous "Leviosa" scene with "mimosa," and you've got me on a Sunday, but with orange juice and champagne levitating toward my mouth and no magic wand in sight.

There's perhaps nothing I look forward to more than brunch, especially when surrounded by breakfast staples such as pancakes, French toast, oatmeal, and, of course, bacon. Friends are okay, too, I guess, but they have to be on board with prioritizing eating and drinking over catching up, though the latter will certainly happen once the buzz kicks in and the hanger subsides.

The beauty of brunch is that it can also take many forms. Outdoors in scarves, inside with drag queens, and, most excitingly, in your own home with these recipes that absolutely won't disappoint, as long as you keep the alcohol flowing to mask the tastes of your potential failures. Kidding. They're legitimately foolproof, so much so that you may not want to make them often or your basic besties will be inviting themselves over all the time.

5

Holy Crepes

PREP TIME: 20 MINUTES   **COOK TIME:** 30 MINUTES PLUS CHILLING
TOTAL TIME: 50 MINUTES PLUS CHILLING
YIELD: 12 SWEET OR SAVORY CREPES (4 TO 6 SERVINGS)

One of my lowest of all lows as a food editor was being assigned the story "Where do hot dogs come from?" This led me to question the value of my Northwestern education, as well as my entire existence. Most unfortunately, it also led to an entire weekend of contemplating a career change, from which I distracted myself with nonstop cooking sessions. For this particular mental breakdown, my brain was sponsored by crepes—the French delicacy that you can stuff with literally anything you find in your apartment. The real winners, for me, were ingredients such as Nutella (duh) and pancetta (double duh), which are obvious basic bitch standouts. But feel free to experiment and layer your thin pancakes with anything that will prevent irrational decision-making or an unscheduled trip to the psychiatrist.

1   First make the crepes: In a blender, combine the flour, sugar, salt, milk, eggs, and butter and blend until smooth, 1 minute. Refrigerate the mixture for at least 1 hour or up to overnight.

2   Heat a small nonstick pan over medium heat. Using a pastry brush, lightly coat the bottom and sides of the pan with butter. Give the batter a quick stir, then, using a ¼-cup ladle, pour 1 ladleful of the crepe batter into the pan, swirling the pan to make a thin, even layer. Cook until the crepe is set and lightly golden, 1 to 2 minutes. Using a small offset spatula, lift up the edge of the crepe and use your fingers to flip the crepe over, then cook for an additional 30 seconds. Transfer to a plate and repeat with the remaining batter, adding more butter to the pan as needed. You should have about 12 crepes.

3   To make the sweet version, place a crepe on a clean work surface. Spread 2 tablespoons of the chocolate-hazelnut spread over the crepe. Top with 2 tablespoons of the sliced strawberries and fold the other half of the crepe over the toppings, then fold the crepe in half again, creating a triangle. Repeat with the remaining crepes. Drizzle with honey and sprinkle with confectioners' sugar before serving.

To make the savory version, in a small nonstick skillet, cook the pancetta until the fat has rendered and the pancetta is golden brown, about 5 minutes. Transfer to a paper towel–lined plate.

Place a crepe on a clean work surface. Spread 1 tablespoon of the apricot jam over the crepe. Top half of the crepe with a few slices of the Brie. Top the Brie with apple slices, pancetta, arugula, and chives. Fold the other half of the crepe over the toppings and then fold the crepe in half again creating a triangle. Repeat with the remaining crepes. Serve warm, garnished with chives.

FOR THE CREPES

1 cup all-purpose flour

2 teaspoons granulated sugar

¹/₂ teaspoon kosher salt

1¹/₂ cups whole milk, at room temperature

4 eggs, at room temperature

4 tablespoons unsalted butter, plus more for brushing

FOR THE SWEET VERSION

1¹/₂ cups chocolate-hazelnut spread

1¹/₂ cups sliced strawberries (about 10 ounces)

Honey, for drizzling

Confectioners' sugar, for dusting

FOR THE SAVORY VERSION

³/₄ pound pancetta, cut into ¹/₄-inch cubes

³/₄ cup apricot jam

12 ounces Brie cheese, thinly sliced

2 Granny Smith apples, peeled, cored, and thinly sliced

3 cups arugula

³/₄ cup chopped fresh chives, plus more for garnish

JUST THE TIPS

Crepes can be stored, stacked between layers of wax paper in a zip-top bag, in the refrigerator for up to 5 days or in the freezer for up to 1 month.

FOR THE PIE CRUST

2 cups all-purpose flour

1¹/₂ teaspoons salt

1 teaspoon sugar

1 stick unsalted butter, cut into
    ¹/₂-inch pieces and chilled

6 to 7 tablespoons ice water

FOR THE FILLING

8 ounces bacon, cut crosswise
    into ¹/₄-inch-wide strips
    (5 pieces)

2 medium shallots, peeled
    and thinly sliced

3 cups packed chopped fresh
    baby spinach

4 ounces Gruyère cheese,
    grated (1 cup)

1 cup half-and-half

1 cup cottage cheese

4 eggs, beaten

2 egg yolks, beaten

¹/₂ teaspoon kosher salt

¹/₄ teaspoon freshly ground
    black pepper

¹/₄ teaspoon cayenne pepper

JUST THE TIPS

Quiche is the perfect make-
ahead dish. It can be served
warm or at room temperature.

THE MORE YOU GLOW

The cottage cheese adds
25 grams of protein to the
quiche!

A Not-Disappointing Quiche

PREP TIME: 40 MINUTES   **COOK TIME:** 2 HOURS PLUS CHILLING
TOTAL TIME: 2 HOURS 40 MINUTES PLUS CHILLING   **YIELD:** 6 TO 8 SERVINGS

When it comes to most store-bought quiches, you go into eating with the expectation of excitement but ultimately end up disappointed, much like the time I ordered what I thought to be a life-size Lucite chair for my apartment. Instead, and to everyone else's amusement, it turned out to be a plastic replica for a dollhouse. (I still own it because it makes an amazing conversation starter for all of these nondates I'm having.) Quiche doesn't have to be a dollhouse chair. In fact, quiche can be a mother-effin' chair from Versailles, adorned with the flakiness, moistness, and flavor you'd expect from shamelessly spending $10-plus on something that ends up tasting like crap. Eat your heart out, Marie Antoinette.

1   First make the pie crust: In a food processor, combine the flour, salt, and sugar. Pulse to combine. Add the butter and pulse until the butter is broken down into pea-size pieces. Slowly drizzle in the water while pulsing until the dough just comes together. On a clean work surface, gather the dough together and form it into a disk. Wrap the dough in plastic wrap and refrigerate for at least 30 minutes.

2   Preheat the oven to 375°F.

3   Place the dough on a lightly floured work surface and roll it out into a 14-inch round. Transfer the dough to a 9-inch deep-dish pie plate, allowing the excess dough to hang off the edges. Trim the overhanging dough to 1 inch. Fold the dough under itself and crimp the edges. Chill in the fridge for 15 minutes. Line the dough with parchment paper and fill with pie weights or dried beans. Bake for 20 minutes. Remove the parchment and the weights or beans and bake for 15 minutes longer, until golden in color. Remove the crust from the oven and let cool completely before adding the filling.

4   Meanwhile, make the filling: In a large nonstick pan, cook the bacon over medium-high heat until golden brown, 7 minutes. Add the shallots and cook until translucent and beginning to color, 4 minutes. Drain the excess bacon fat. Return the pan to the heat, add the spinach, and sauté until wilted, 3 minutes. Remove from the heat and set aside to cool.

5   Spread the Gruyère over the bottom of the cooled pie crust. Top with the cooled bacon mixture.

6   In a medium bowl, beat the half-and-half, cottage cheese, eggs, and egg yolks to combine. Season with the salt and black pepper. Pour the egg mixture into the pie crust and sprinkle the top with the cayenne. Bake until the edges are set but the center still jiggles, 1 hour to 1 hour 15 minutes. Let cool on a wire rack for at least 1 hour before serving.

You Own Everything Bagel with Lox

PREP TIME: 20 MINUTES   **TOTAL TIME:** 20 MINUTES   **YIELD:** 4 SERVINGS

1 (8-ounce) container whipped cream cheese

2 tablespoons chopped fresh dill, plus more for garnish

2 tablespoons chopped fresh chives

4 everything bagels, halved and toasted

1 (8-ounce) package lox

2 Persian cucumbers, thinly sliced

2 tomatoes on the vine, sliced

1/2 red onion, thinly sliced

2 tablespoons capers

1 lemon, cut into wedges, for serving

Tourists in New York seem to celebrate National Walk as Slow as You Can Day every day, which makes early morning commutes just the best (extreme sarcasm). But if I'm walking down the busy streets with an everything bagel and lox in hand, you'd think I was Mary Poppins floating from block to block with an umbrella in tow and zero effs to give. Now that I'm showing you how to re-create this Disney-level magic in your own kitchen (and for a crowd!), you'll also be skipping around your city as if you've won the lottery or licked a hallucinogenic toad. I'm not sure what it feels like to experience either one of these scenarios, but they're highs I'd welcome if they induce any feeling remotely similar to an everything bagel with lox.

1   In a medium bowl, stir together the cream cheese, dill, and chives to combine.

2   On a large platter, arrange the bagels, lox, cucumbers, tomatoes, onion, capers, and lemon wedges next to the bowl of cream cheese and a small dish of dill for garnish. Allow guests to build their own bagels.

Cha-Cha-Cha Chia Pudding

PREP TIME: 5 MINUTES
TOTAL TIME: 5 MINUTES PLUS CHILLING OVERNIGHT
YIELD: 4 SERVINGS

Chia seeds remind me of the Orbitz drinks we coveted in the 1990s. We enjoyed them because they resembled lava lamps, not because they tasted good. Like the unidentifiable gelatinous globules that now exist only in our dreams, chia seeds are flavorless and only as good as the ingredients that surround them. When soaked overnight in milk (or a milk alternative) and infused with a sweetener, they create a texture play that is totally tubular, with toppings such as coconut and kiwi that also lend themselves to even more taste and texture complexities. If only my hair would grow as fast as an actual chia plant, then this would truly be the miracle food we've all been waiting for.

1 cup unsweetened vanilla coconut milk

1 cup coconut yogurt

2 tablespoons pure maple syrup

1 teaspoon vanilla extract

Pinch of kosher salt

$1/2$ cup chia seeds

1 green kiwi, peeled and sliced

1 SunGold yellow kiwi, peeled and sliced

$1/2$ cup pomegranate seeds

$1/2$ cup unsweetened coconut flakes, toasted

---

1 In a large bowl, whisk together the vanilla coconut milk, coconut yogurt, maple syrup, vanilla extract, and salt until combined. Whisk in the chia seeds, cover with plastic wrap, and refrigerate overnight.

2 Spoon the chia pudding into four small glasses for serving. Top with kiwi slices, pomegranate seeds, and coconut. Serve.

THE MORE YOU GLOW
Chia seeds are packed with omega-3s, antioxidants, and lots of fiber. This pudding will keep you full!

LITERALLY CAN'T EVEN
If you like a sweeter breakfast, add an additional tablespoon of maple syrup. The coconut yogurt adds an extra layer of creaminess to this chia pudding, but remove it if you're not a fan.

I Can Açai Clearly Now Bowl

PREP TIME: 10 MINUTES   **COOK TIME:** 2 MINUTES
TOTAL TIME: 12 MINUTES   **YIELD:** 3 CUPS

My favorite berry will always be one that can be turned into wine. Despite this glaring shortcoming, açai is slowly inching its way to the top with a frozen ice cream–esque preparation and assortment of healthy and customizable toppings. Plus, it has a pretty purple hue, which gives me yet another excuse to wave my gay flag loud and proud so that the homophobes in the back can see and taste it. The fact that it's served in a bowl is the cherry on top, as we basics have come to appreciate. Don't let this stop you from adding an actual cherry, though, which can convince you, if only for a second, that it's an ice cream sundae and not something that's surprisingly healthy for you.

1   Place two serving bowls in the freezer to chill.

2   In a blender, combine the açai puree, vanilla coconut milk, strawberries, dates, banana, flaxseed, and maca powder. Process until smooth.

3   Pour into the chilled bowls and garnish with cocoa nibs, strawberries, blueberries, bananas, and almonds. Serve immediately.

BASIC BASICS

Açai berries are a Brazilian superfruit native to the Amazon. They taste like a cross between blackberries and unsweetened chocolate. Whole berries are hard to find, but you can buy frozen açai puree, açai powder, and açai juice.

1 (3.5-ounce) package frozen unsweetened açai puree, slightly thawed
$^{1}/_{2}$ cup vanilla coconut milk
$1^{1}/_{2}$ cups frozen strawberries
2 Medjool dates, pitted
1 banana, cut into thirds
1 tablespoon flaxseeds
1 teaspoon maca powder

FOR TOPPINGS
Cacao nibs
Fresh strawberries, sliced
Fresh blueberries
Banana, sliced
Sliced almonds, toasted

THE MORE YOU GLOW
Açai berries are loaded with antioxidants, with three times the antioxidants than blueberries.

Gossip-Worthy Sunday Pancakes

PREP TIME: 15 MINUTES   **COOK TIME:** 30 MINUTES
TOTAL TIME: 45 MINUTES   **YIELD:** 10 PANCAKES

If Sunday is God's day, then God clearly wants us to partake in boozy brunch activities and gossip about everyone we know. He also clearly wants us to nosh on pancakes that soak up all the rosé and liquor so that we don't waste a sick day on Monday. Every breakfast table demands a pancake, and while they come in all shapes, sizes, and preparations, these are the ones that will have you bidding adieu to Jenny Craig and saying hello to layering season. I also can't believe I'm saying this, but maple syrup is completely optional, much like my dignity after a late-night rager at a local dive bar (which we'll surely be discussing at any brunch with pancakes).

FOR THE BLUEBERRY SYRUP

2 cups frozen wild blueberries (8 ounces)

1/3 cup honey

1 cup water

1 tablespoon tapioca starch

2 tablespoons freshly squeezed lemon juice (from 1 medium lemon)

FOR THE PANCAKES

2 cups all-purpose flour

1 1/2 teaspoon baking powder

1/2 teaspoon baking soda

1/2 teaspoon ground cinnamon

1 teaspoon kosher salt

2 tablespoons sugar

2 eggs

1 3/4 cups buttermilk

1 teaspoon vanilla extract

4 tablespoons unsalted butter, melted and cooled, plus 2 tablespoons unsalted butter for cooking the pancakes

JUST THE TIPS

If you aren't serving these right away, heat the oven to 200°F and keep the pancakes warm on a baking sheet for up to 20 minutes.

Store blueberry syrup in the fridge in an airtight container for up to 2 weeks.

1   First make the blueberry syrup: In a medium saucepan, combine the blueberries, honey, and water and bring to a boil. Reduce the heat to maintain a simmer and cook for 10 minutes.

2   In a small bowl, whisk together the tapioca starch and lemon juice to combine. Remove the blueberries from the heat and add the tapioca starch mixture. Stir to combine until the sauce thickens. Set aside.

3   Make the pancakes: In a large bowl, mix the flour, baking powder, baking soda, cinnamon, salt, and sugar. In a medium bowl, whisk together the eggs, buttermilk, vanilla, and melted butter to combine. Stir the wet ingredients into the dry ingredients, mixing to combine. The batter should be a little lumpy.

4   On a griddle or in a large nonstick skillet over medium-low heat, melt 1 tablespoon of the butter. Using a 1/3-cup measure, ladle the batter into the pan to form 5 pancakes (or as many as will fit in the pan). Cook until the edges set and air bubbles begin to rise to the surface, flip, and cook for 2 more minutes, until cooked through and golden brown. Transfer the pancake to a plate and repeat with the remaining batter, using the remaining 1 tablespoon butter to grease the pan between batches. Serve warm, with the blueberry syrup.

FOR THE MAQUI BERRY COMPOTE

¹/₂ cup raspberries

³/₄ cup sliced strawberries

¹/₂ cup blueberries

¹/₄ cup sugar

2 tablespoons freshly squeezed lemon juice (from 1 medium lemon)

2 teaspoons maqui powder

FOR THE PARFAIT

1 cup plain whole-milk Greek yogurt

1 cup Brooklyn Hipster–Approved Granola (page 191)

1 teaspoon honey

JUST THE TIPS

Additional maqui berry compote can be stored in an airtight container in the refrigerator for up to 2 weeks.

If making ahead, wait to add the granola until ready to serve. Refrigerating the granola can cause it to lose its crunch.

Greek Yogurt Parf-Yay!

PREP TIME: 15 MINUTES   **COOK TIME:** 10 MINUTES PLUS COOLING
TOTAL TIME: 25 MINUTES PLUS COOLING   **YIELD:** 1 SERVING

"Bitch better have my honey"—Rihanna, probably, if she only knew how delicious this parfait tasted with the added sweetness of one of nature's most sacred treasures. Greek yogurt's trendiness continues to reign supreme and, like an ugly birthmark or the decision to get bangs, you better get used to it. It's here to stay for the long run, and why shouldn't it? It's creamy, it's rich, it serves as an excellent base to practically anything, and it offers a fantastic amount of protein. I've also once added chocolate chips, almond extract, almond butter, and oats to create a cookie dough batter–esque option that would make even my judgmental grandmother proud (or at least distract her, temporarily, from asking about grandkids). This parfait, piled high with maqui berry compote and my homemade granola, is also a quick-and-easy breakfast to serve guests who may be visiting or unwelcomingly stopping by. Its pretty presentation gives true meaning to the phrase "Fake it till you make it." Or in this case, "Make it and continue to fake it."

1   First make the maqui berry compote: In a small saucepan, combine the raspberries, strawberries, blueberries, sugar, and lemon juice. Cook over medium heat until the berries begin to break down, 10 minutes. Remove from the heat and stir in the maqui powder. Cool completely.

2   Make the parfait: In a mason jar, layer ½ cup of the yogurt, ¼ cup of the maqui berry compote, and ½ cup of the granola. Repeat to make a second layer of each ingredient. Drizzle with the honey and serve.

Brooklyn Hipster–Approved Granola

PREP TIME: 10 MINUTES   **COOK TIME:** 35 MINUTES
TOTAL TIME: 45 MINUTES PLUS COOLING   **YIELD:** 10 CUPS

I once typed the word "tits" instead of "its" in an important work email before nine a.m. I also once spilled an entire bowl of Cinnamon Toast Crunch on my keyboard before school. What I'm trying to say is that mornings and I don't mesh well, much like my skin and a cheap polyester blend. But something that makes a typical morning happier? Granola. And not just any granola. This granola with some of my favorite things: pumpkin seeds, oats, and walnuts, which activate the brain function that Ambien stole from me. The beauty of granola is that it can be tossed into anything—yogurt, cookies, trail mix, even pancakes. The ugliness of granola is that it can be tossed into anything, and because it deceptively seems healthy but is actually a gigantic calorie bomb, you can easily be tricked into thinking that your breakfast is light and diet-friendly.

2 1/2 cups rolled oats
1/2 cup uncooked white quinoa
1/2 cup raw hulled pumpkin seeds (pepitas)
1/2 cup walnuts, chopped
3/4 cup unsweetened coconut flakes
1/4 cup wheat germ
1/2 teaspoon ground cinnamon
1 teaspoon kosher salt
1/2 cup coconut oil
1/2 cup pure maple syrup
2 teaspoons vanilla extract
1 egg white
3/4 cup finely chopped dried apricots

1   Preheat the oven to 325°F. Line a baking sheet with parchment paper.

2   In a large bowl, combine the oats, quinoa, pumpkin seeds, walnuts, coconut flakes, wheat germ, cinnamon, and salt. Set aside.

3   In a small saucepan, combine the coconut oil and maple syrup. Bring to a simmer, remove from the heat, and add the vanilla. Stir to combine. Pour over the oat mixture and toss to coat.

4   In a medium bowl, whisk the egg white until light and foamy. Pour over the oat mixture and toss to coat again. Spread the granola over the prepared baking sheet in an even layer, pressing it down.

5   Bake for 30 to 35 minutes, until golden brown and fragrant, rotating the pan halfway through baking. Remove from the oven and let cool completely.

6   Once it's cool, break up the granola, leaving some large clusters. Add the apricots. Store in an airtight container at room temperature for up to 2 weeks or in the freezer for up to 2 months.

French Toast That's Actually Worth the Carb Binge

PREP TIME: 15 MINUTES   **COOK TIME:** 15 MINUTES
TOTAL TIME: 30 MINUTES   **YIELD:** 4 TO 6 SERVINGS

If you can believe it, I actually ran and completed the New York City Marathon. What got me through were carb-laden weekend breakfasts that I would dub as "fuel for my training." While the French toast stayed, the trainings didn't. In fact, the most I ever ran was eight miles (much like Eminem), with many breaks along the way. Adrenaline, stubbornness, and maybe a little bit of Jesus is what got me through the finish line, but certainly not a workout plan or elevated sense of athleticism. The day after the race, medal still clinging to my neck, the first thing I ate was more French toast, which always proved to be the true winner during my "training." Would I ever partake in another marathon again? Maybe,* just so long as I get to continue eating French toast every weekend. (*The only marathons I'll be partaking in are boozy brunches, thanks.)

1   Preheat the oven to 200°F. Line a baking sheet with a wire rack.

2   In a 9 by 13-inch baking dish, whisk together the eggs, milk, cream, vanilla, maple syrup, salt, cinnamon, and nutmeg.

3   Place 2 or 3 slices of the challah into the egg mixture and allow them to soak for about 4 minutes, flipping them halfway through.

4   In a large nonstick skillet over medium heat, melt 1 tablespoon of the butter. Add the soaked challah slices and cook until golden brown on both sides, about 3 minutes per side. Transfer to the prepared baking sheet and keep warm in the oven. Repeat to soak and cook the remaining bread.

5   Serve the French toast with a drizzle of maple syrup, freshly sliced strawberries, and a dusting of confectioners' sugar, if you like. Enjoy.

6 eggs

³/₄ cup whole milk

³/₄ cup heavy cream

1 teaspoon vanilla extract

2 tablespoons maple syrup

³/₄ teaspoon kosher salt

¹/₂ teaspoon ground cinnamon

¹/₈ teaspoon freshly grated nutmeg

¹/₂ loaf challah bread, sliced into 4 to 6 (1-inch-thick) slices

4 tablespoons unsalted butter

Maple syrup, warmed

Fresh strawberries, sliced

Confectioners' sugar, for dusting (optional)

LITERALLY CAN'T EVEN
Don't have challah bread? Feel free to use brioche or a Pullman loaf.

Non-Elderly Oatmeal with Goji Berries

PREP TIME: 10 MINUTES   **COOK TIME:** 20 MINUTES
TOTAL TIME: 30 MINUTES   **YIELD:** 4 SERVINGS

1 cup steel-cut oats

2 cups oat milk

1 cup water

$^1/_2$ teaspoon vanilla extract

1 tablespoon maple syrup

$^1/_2$ teaspoon kosher salt

Ground cinnamon

2 tablespoons hulled hemp
seeds

$^1/_2$ cup goji berries

$^1/_2$ cup raw hulled pumpkin
seeds (pepitas)

Dinosaur oatmeal was essentially my first introduction to science. How did the eggs disappear to reveal sprinkle dino children? Why do the T. rex and triceratops on the box literally salivate over the idea of eating their babies? It's a lot to take in, but truly defined a pivotal state of my childhood development. While dinosaur oatmeal isn't appropriate in adulthood (actually, I take that back: it's always appropriate), you can liven up standard oatmeal with an impressive array of healthy ingredients such as goji berries and hemp seeds to take it from nursing home staple to "Ohhhh, child, are you Chef Girlardee?" levels of yum.

1   In a medium skillet over medium-high heat, toast the oats until fragrant, about 4 minutes. Remove from the heat and set aside.

2   In a medium saucepot, combine the oat milk, water, and vanilla. Bring to a simmer. Reduce the heat to low and add the oats. Cook at a low simmer, stirring occasionally, until the oats have absorbed the liquid, the mixture has thickened, and the oats are tender, about 20 minutes. Stir in the maple syrup and salt. Remove from the heat.

3   Scoop the oatmeal into bowls and garnish with a sprinkling of cinnamon, the hemp seeds, goji berries, and pumpkin seeds. Serve.

LITERALLY CAN'T EVEN
The oat milk adds a little extra creaminess and enhances
the oat flavor, but feel free to use any milk you desire,
including coconut milk, nut milk, or cow's milk.

Sweet, Spice, and Pretty Damn Nice Chicken and Waffles with a Homemade Biscuit

FOR THE SPICY FRIED CHICKEN

1 cup buttermilk

2 tablespoons hot sauce

4 bone-in, skin-on chicken thighs

4 chicken drumsticks

Kosher salt and freshly ground black pepper

Vegetable oil, for frying

2 teaspoons seasoned salt (like Lawry's)

2 teaspoons garlic powder

2¹/₂ teaspoons cayenne pepper

³/₄ cup all-purpose flour

³/₄ cup rice flour

¹/₂ cup cornstarch

1 teaspoon baking powder

2 tablespoons dark brown sugar

1 teaspoon hot smoked paprika

1 tablespoon chili powder

PREP TIME: 50 MINUTES   **COOK TIME:** 50 MINUTES
TOTAL TIME: 1 HOUR 40 MINUTES PLUS MARINATING
YIELD: 4 TO 6 SERVINGS

If loving canned biscuits is wrong, then I don't want to be right. And if you are what you eat, then I'm hot and spicy. But also a chicken. (You can't have it all.) One of my favorite breakfast indulgences is spicy fried chicken served on waffles with a biscuit. Homemade biscuits aren't necessary, but because it's in our innate basic bitch nature to impress everyone we come into contact with, I'm offering a recipe that puts your favorite breakfast spot's biscuits to shame. Yeah, I'm looking at you, Cracker Barrel (even though I'll always be here for your cinnamon-forward Old Country Store). Top these bad boys with angelic syrup for a sweet escape that will almost allow you to forgive the South for its plethora of sometimes true stereotypes.

1   First make the spicy fried chicken: In a gallon-size zip-top bag, combine the buttermilk and hot sauce. Season the chicken with salt and black pepper and add to the buttermilk. Marinate in the refrigerator for at least 1 hour and up to overnight.

2   Fill a large Dutch oven with 3 inches of vegetable oil and heat the oil to 365°F. Line a baking sheet with a wire rack.

3   In a large bowl, combine the seasoned salt, 1 teaspoon of the garlic powder, ¹/₂ teaspoon of the cayenne, the all-purpose flour, rice flour, cornstarch, and baking powder. Add a few tablespoons of the buttermilk marinade and mix to create clumps. This will help make the chicken extra crispy.

4   Remove the chicken from the buttermilk marinade and dredge the pieces one at a time in the flour mixture. Dip back in the buttermilk and then the flour mixture again, creating a double dredge. A few pieces at a time, add the chicken to the hot oil and cook until golden brown and the internal temperature reaches 165°F, 6 to 8 minutes, flipping halfway through. Transfer to the prepared baking sheet and season with salt. Repeat to fry the remaining chicken. Set the frying pan aside to cool.

5 In a large bowl, whisk together the remaining 2 teaspoons cayenne, the remaining 1 teaspoon garlic powder, the dark brown sugar, paprika, and the chili powder. Whisk in 1 cup of the frying oil until combined. Using a pastry brush, brush the fried chicken with the spicy oil. Keep the cooked chicken in a warm oven until ready to serve.

6 Next, make the cheddar-chive biscuits: Preheat the oven to 350°F.

7 In a large bowl, whisk together the flour, granulated sugar, baking powder, and salt. Using a pastry cutter or your fingertips, blend in the butter until it is broken down into pea-size pieces. Add the cheddar and chives and mix to combine. Add the buttermilk and stir until the dough just comes together.

8 Turn the dough out onto a lightly floured surface and press it into a 6-inch square. Cut it into nine 2-inch squares. Brush with the melted butter and bake for 20 to 25 minutes.

9 Meanwhile, make the waffles: Line a baking sheet with a wire rack. Heat a waffle iron according to the manufacturer's instructions.

10 In a large bowl, whisk together the flour, granulated sugar, baking powder, salt, and cinnamon. In another large bowl, whisk together the milk, vanilla, eggs yolks, and melted butter.

11 In the bowl of a stand mixer fitted with the whisk attachment, beat the egg whites until they hold stiff peaks, about 3 minutes. Fold the milk–egg yolk mixture into the flour mixture until fully combined. Fold in the egg whites, making sure they are combined; do not overmix.

12 Coat your waffle iron with nonstick spray. Scoop ½ cup of the batter into the waffle iron and cook according to the manufacturer's instructions until golden brown and cooked through, 3 to 4 minutes. Transfer to the prepared baking sheet and keep warm in the oven. Repeat with the remaining batter.

13 To serve, place 2 waffles on each plate and top with slices of butter and maple syrup. Add a chicken thigh, a drumstick, and a biscuit to each plate. Serve.

FOR THE CHEDDAR-CHIVE BISCUITS

2 cups all-purpose flour

2 tablespoons granulated sugar

1 tablespoon baking powder

1½ teaspoons kosher salt

1½ sticks cold unsalted butter, cut into small pieces

8 ounces extra-sharp cheddar cheese, finely grated (1½ cups)

3 tablespoons chopped fresh chives

¾ cup buttermilk, cold

2 tablespoons unsalted butter, melted

FOR THE WAFFLES

2 cups all-purpose flour

¼ cup granulated sugar

1 tablespoon baking powder

1 teaspoon kosher salt

½ teaspoon ground cinnamon

1½ cups whole milk

2 teaspoons vanilla extract

3 eggs, separated

1 stick unsalted butter, melted, plus room-temperature butter for serving

Maple syrup, for serving

JUST THE TIPS

The unbaked biscuits can be frozen for up to 3 months in a zip-top bag before baking. If you're baking from frozen, add about 5 minutes to the baking time.

An Egg-cellent Guide That Can't Be Beat

Eggs: You're wanting to freeze, fertilize, or eat them, and while I can't help you with the first two, the last can be achieved through dozens of unique recipes. Whether you're craving a healthy omelet; a bacon, egg, and cheese sandwich; or a classic Benedict, the world's most versatile protein is here for you, to elevate your mood and provide you with sustenance like a true sister. The only problem is picking just one preparation and sticking to it. Or don't: Eat them all and "egg-statically" throw yourself an "eggs-travaganza" while only partially hating yourself for using such terrible puns.

BEC Sando for a Crowd

PREP TIME: 10 MINUTES **COOK TIME:** 20 MINUTES
TOTAL TIME: 30 MINUTES **YIELD:** 6 SANDWICHES

1 Preheat the oven to 350°F. Line a 9 by 13-inch rimmed baking sheet with parchment paper, leaving a 2-inch overhang on two sides. Grease with nonstick spray.

2 Put the bacon on a separate baking sheet and bake until crispy, about 20 minutes.

3 In a large bowl, whisk together the eggs and season with salt and pepper. Pour onto the prepared baking sheet. Carefully transfer to the oven alongside the bacon and bake the eggs for 12 to 15 minutes until set.

4 Meanwhile, heat a large nonstick skillet over medium heat. Add 1 tablespoon of the butter and begin toasting the bread on one side. Transfer to a baking sheet and repeat with the remaining bread, adding 1 tablespoon of butter after every two slices.

5 Remove the eggs and bacon from the oven. Reduce the oven temperature to 200°F.

6 Drain the bacon on paper towels. Invert the eggs onto a cutting board and discard the parchment paper. Top the eggs with the cheese slices and cut into 6 squares. Put an egg square on a piece of toasted bread. Top with 2 slices of cooked bacon and sandwich with another piece of bread. Repeat with the remaining ingredients until you have 6 sandwiches. Place the egg sandwiches in the oven to keep warm until ready to serve.

12 slices extra-thick-cut bacon

12 eggs

Kosher salt and freshly ground black pepper

6 tablespoons unsalted butter

12 slices sourdough Pullman bread or brioche bread

12 slices yellow American cheese

JUST THE TIPS

This is a quick-and-easy way to make BEC sandwiches for a crowd! Keep the sandwiches in a 200°F oven until ready to serve. Even your last rising houseguest will get a warm breakfast sandwich.

Healthy Herbed Omelet

PREP TIME: 20 MINUTES **COOK TIME:** 15 MINUTES
TOTAL TIME: 35 MINUTES **YIELD:** 1 SERVING

2 tablespoons avocado oil

¹/₂ cup cremini mushrooms, sliced

1 garlic clove, minced

1 small shallot, minced

1 cup baby spinach

Kosher salt and freshly ground black pepper

3 egg whites

1 egg

2 tablespoons whole milk

1 tablespoon finely chopped fresh flat-leaf parsley

1 tablespoon finely chopped fresh chives, plus more for garnish

1 teaspoon finely chopped fresh dill

JUST THE TIPS

Make sure to drain the spinach after cooking to avoid excess liquid in your omelet.

If calories aren't a concern, add goat cheese for some tartness or Parmesan for some saltiness.

1   In a medium nonstick skillet over medium-high heat, heat 1 tablespoon of the avocado oil. Add the cremini mushrooms and sauté until golden brown, about 6 minutes. Add the garlic and shallot and cook until translucent, 2 minutes. Add the baby spinach and cook until the spinach wilts and the water cooks out, 5 minutes. Season with salt and pepper. Transfer to a paper towel–lined plate and set aside.

2   In a medium bowl, whisk together the eggs whites, egg, and milk until light and frothy. Add the parsley, chives, and dill. Season with salt.

3   In the same skillet, heat the remaining 1 tablespoon avocado oil over medium heat. Add the egg mixture and swirl it around the pan. Gently stir the egg mixture with a rubber spatula, then swirl the pan, spreading the eggs around the sides of the pan. Reduce the heat to low and cook until the egg is mostly set. Add the mushroom-spinach mixture to the middle of the eggs. Fold the omelet in thirds by tilting the pan and helping the top of the omelet roll over the center and onto a serving plate. Garnish with chopped chives. Serve immediately.

Eggs Benedict 101

Eggs Benedict is made up of English muffins, halved and toasted, Canadian bacon warmed in a skillet, poached eggs, and hollandaise sauce. Two out of the four ingredients are store-bought, so while this dish may appear intimidating, it's actually rather easy to prepare for guests with these simple tips.

When poaching eggs, you want to have water at a simmer in a saucepan with a splash of distilled white vinegar. Adding vinegar makes the whites set faster, resulting in a set white and a runny yolk.

If you want extra-fancy-looking eggs, you can strain your egg whites through a small fine-mesh sieve. This will get rid of any old egg whites that will sauce those strings that hang on to the end of your perfectly poached egg.

If poaching eggs for a crowd, always have an ice bath ready to stop the cooking process. The most important part of a poached egg is the runny yolk, so make sure it doesn't overcook! The eggs can be reheated for about 30 seconds in warm water, drained on a paper towel, and then added to the plate.

A quick-and-easy way to make hollandaise is by using a blender! Simply combine egg yolks, lemon juice, salt, and cayenne in a blender and blend. With the blender running, add melted butter very slowly so that the sauce emulsifies. Adding warm melted butter too quickly will cause your eggs to cook and your hollandaise to look curdled.

For best results, use hollandaise immediately. However, you can hold the sauce for up to 1 hour before using. Simply put the sauce in a heatproof bowl, cover with plastic wrap, and set it over a pot of barely simmering water.

One Hot Pair: Buttermilk Currant Scones with Homemade Raspberry Jam

PREP TIME: 25 MINUTES **COOK TIME:** 40 MINUTES PLUS COOLING
TOTAL TIME: 1 HOUR 5 MINUTES PLUS COOLING **YIELD:** 8 SCONES

When two become one, you don't get just an amazing Spice Girls song. Scones and jam go together like peas and carrots, except way less disgusting. And ever since I rocked a yin-yang necklace in second grade, my life is all about balance. This dynamic duo is something I can house at Guinness World Record levels of consumption, which can be said about pretty much everything in this book. The only difference is that scones are way too easy on the palate, as if you're swallowing pillows of layered goodness. And for someone who is in a chronic state of sleep deprivation, swallowing pillows (and not pills) apparently resonates with me. (If I can't sleep on them, I may as well eat them, right?)

1 Preheat the oven to 375°F. Line a baking sheet with parchment paper.

2 First make the raspberry jam: In a small saucepan, combine the raspberries, sugar, lemon juice, and salt. Bring to a boil over high heat, stirring until the sugar has dissolved. Skim off any light-colored foam around the sides and discard. Cook, stirring occasionally, until thickened and the temperature reaches 220°F, 12 to 15 minutes. Remove from the heat. Strain through a fine-mesh sieve to remove some or all of the seeds, if desired. Ladle into a mason jar and cool completely.

3 Make the scones: In a large bowl, combine the cake flour, baking powder, baking soda, salt, and granulated sugar. Add the butter and, using a pastry blender or your fingers, blend the butter into the flour until it is in pea-size pieces. Create a well in the center of the bowl and add the eggs, buttermilk, and vanilla. Using a fork, mix the ingredients until they are just combined into a shaggy dough. Add the currants, if using, and knead until combined.

4 Lightly flour a work surface and roll the dough out into a 1-inch-thick round using a rolling pin. Cut into 8 wedges. Put the wedges on the prepared baking sheet. Brush with buttermilk and sprinkle with raw sugar.

5 Bake for 20 to 25 minutes, until golden brown and crisp. Serve warm, with the raspberry jam.

FOR THE RASPBERRY JAM

3 cups fresh raspberries

1½ cups granulated sugar

1 tablespoon freshly squeezed lemon juice (from 1 medium lemon)

¼ teaspoon kosher salt

FOR THE SCONES

3 cups cake flour, plus more for dusting

1 tablespoon baking powder

½ teaspoon baking soda

1 teaspoon kosher salt

¼ cup granulated sugar

1 stick unsalted butter, cut into ½-inch pieces and chilled

2 eggs

½ cup buttermilk, plus more for brushing

1 teaspoon vanilla extract

½ cup dried currants (optional)

Raw sugar, for sprinkling

JUST THE TIPS

The raspberry jam will keep in the jar in the fridge for up to 1 month. Freeze your scones before baking for a quick make-ahead treat. Simply take the scones out of the freezer while the oven is preheating and place on a baking sheet. Add a couple of minutes to the baking time to account for the scones being partially frozen.

Lumberjack Boyfriend–Approved Apple Cider Doughnuts

PREP TIME: 20 MINUTES **COOK TIME:** 25 MINUTES
TOTAL TIME: 45 MINUTES PLUS COOLING **YIELD:** 12 DOUGHNUTS

1¹/₂ cups apple cider

1²/₃ cups all-purpose flour

1¹/₂ teaspoons baking powder

1¹/₄ teaspoons kosher salt

2 teaspoons ground cinnamon

¹/₄ teaspoon freshly grated nutmeg

1 stick unsalted butter, at room temperature, plus 1 stick unsalted butter, melted

1 cup packed light brown sugar

1 cup granulated sugar

2 eggs, at room temperature

1 teaspoon vanilla extract

JUST THE TIPS

These doughnuts make buying a doughnut pan worth it. No need to go to the apple orchard for fresh apple cider doughnuts this year!

For added apple flavor, we've cooked down the apple cider into an apple cider concentrate to get the most bang for our buck.

The arrival of apple cider doughnut season is meant to be sung from the rooftops at Kesha "Praying" scream-note levels of enthusiasm. They're the sole reason why you dress your boyfriend up as a lumberjack and bring him to an orchard, other than Instagram opportunities, of course. I'm not sure what it is about the hot, flaky, sugary bag that can probably solve world peace or decode the root cause of Lana del Rey's many moods (which I relate to oh-so-much), but I'm always here for it, first in line, weathering the elements of public transportation to get there. On the off chance I'm not willing to make the trek north from Manhattan, this recipe totally suffices. Just be sure to document your efforts on social media, or it may not be worth the effort.

1 Preheat the oven to 350°F. Grease two 6-cavity doughnut pans with nonstick spray.

2 In a small saucepan, heat the apple cider over high heat until it has reduced to ¹/₂ cup, about 10 minutes. Cool completely.

3 In a large bowl, whisk together the flour, baking powder, salt, 1 teaspoon of the cinnamon, and the nutmeg to combine.

4 In the bowl of a stand mixer fitted with the paddle attachment, cream the butter, light brown sugar, and ¹/₂ cup of the granulated sugar until light and fluffy, about 4 minutes. Add the eggs, one at a time, beating well after each addition. Add the vanilla and beat to combine. On low speed, add half of the flour mixture, followed by the reduced apple cider. Add the remaining flour mixture and beat until the batter comes together.

5 Transfer the batter to a large piping bag and pipe it into the prepared doughnut pans so the cavities are about two-thirds full. Bake until golden brown and cooked through, 12 to 15 minutes, rotating the pans halfway through. Remove from the oven and let cool in the pans for 10 minutes. Transfer to a wire rack set over a baking sheet.

6 In a shallow bowl, combine the remaining ¹/₂ cup granulated sugar and the remaining 1 teaspoon cinnamon. Brush the doughnuts all over with the melted butter and dip them into the cinnamon-sugar mixture, coating the doughnuts fully. Serve immediately.

Cinnamon Rolls with Stupid Amounts of Cream Cheese Frosting

PREP TIME: 40 MINUTES **COOK TIME:** 35 MINUTES
TOTAL TIME: 1 HOUR 15 MINUTES PLUS RISING
YIELDS: 9 JUMBO OR 18 REGULAR CINNAMON ROLLS

1 cup warm water (between 105 and 115°F)

2 (¼-ounce) envelopes active dry yeast (4½ teaspoons)

1 cup granulated sugar

5 tablespoons plus 1 stick unsalted butter, melted

2 teaspoons vanilla extract

1 egg, at room temperature, beaten

3¾ cups all-purpose flour

1 teaspoon kosher salt

½ cup packed light brown sugar

2 tablespoons ground cinnamon

½ teaspoon kosher salt

FOR THE ICING

8 ounces cream cheese, at room temperature

4 tablespoons unsalted butter, at room temperature

1 cup confectioners' sugar

2 teaspoons vanilla extract

2 tablespoons whole milk

Pinch of kosher salt

They say there's nothing like a well-balanced, nutritious breakfast to start your day, to which I say, "To hell with that." Breakfast is the best excuse to eat dishes that are practically dessert, all before ten a.m. and minus the guilt. Cinnamon rolls are a gooey and excellent way to ignore the food pyramid and go hog wild on cream cheese frosting, which, frankly, should cover the entire food pyramid. Because have you eaten anything that doesn't taste better with more cream cheese frosting? No, you haven't.

1   In the bowl of a stand mixer fitted with the dough hook, combine the warm water, yeast, and 2 tablespoons of the granulated sugar. Let stand for 5 minutes, until the yeast is frothy. Add 5 tablespoons of the melted butter, the vanilla, and the egg and mix to combine.

2   In a large bowl, stir together the flour, 6 tablespoons of the granulated sugar, and the salt to combine. With the mixer on low speed, gradually add the flour mixture and mix until the dough pulls away from the side of the bowl and forms a ball, about 5 minutes. Continue to mix until the dough is shiny and elastic, about 5 minutes. Transfer the dough to a greased bowl and let rise in a warm spot until doubled in size, about 1 hour.

3   Meanwhile, in a medium bowl, combine the remaining ½ cup granulated sugar with the light brown sugar, cinnamon, and salt. Set aside.

4   Grease a 12-inch cast-iron skillet with nonstick spray.

5   On a lightly floured surface, roll out the dough to a 16 by 14-inch rectangle. Depending on the climate, you may need to add additional flour to make the dough thicker. Spread the remaining melted butter over the surface of the dough and sprinkle with the cinnamon-sugar mixture. Starting from one long side, roll the dough into a tight log. Cut a 1-foot-long piece of unflavored dental floss. Slide it under the cinnamon roll log and cross the ends over the top to cut the log into 2½-inch-thick rolls. If you do not have floss, use a serrated knife, wiping the blade clean after each cut.

6   Place the cinnamon rolls in the prepared cast-iron skillet and cover with plastic wrap. Let rise in a warm place for 30 minutes.

7   Preheat the oven to 325°F.

8   Bake the cinnamon rolls for 45 minutes, until cooked through. Remove from the oven and let rest for 10 minutes.

9   Meanwhile, make the icing: In the bowl of a stand mixer fitted with the paddle attachment, beat the cream cheese and butter until combined. Gradually add the confectioners' sugar, vanilla, milk, and salt and beat until light and fluffy.

10 Spread the icing over the cinnamon rolls and serve warm.

LITERALLY CAN'T EVEN

Make these cinnamon rolls your own. Switch up the spices by adding some ground coriander, ginger, or nutmeg. Fold in some orange zest for a fresh kick, or top with chopped nuts or dried fruits. And who could forget chocolate!

JUST THE TIPS

If you prefer a smaller cinnamon roll, simply cut the rolls into 1-inch pieces, use two 12-inch cast-iron skillets, and bake for 35 minutes.

Blue-Ribbon Blueberry Muffins

PREP TIME: 20 MINUTES   **COOK TIME:** 35 MINUTES
TOTAL TIME: 55 MINUTES PLUS COOLING   **YIELD:** 16 MUFFINS

1 1/2 cups all-purpose flour

1 cup whole-wheat flour

1 1/2 teaspoons baking powder

1 teaspoon baking soda

1 1/2 teaspoons kosher salt

1 stick unsalted butter,
    at room temperature

1 1/4 cups granulated sugar

3 eggs, at room temperature

2 teaspoons vanilla extract

1 teaspoon finely grated lemon
    zest

1 teaspoon freshly squeezed
    lemon juice

3/4 cup sour cream

1/2 cup buttermilk

2 cups fresh blueberries

Raw sugar, for sprinkling

JUST THE TIPS

If you want to be really fussy, you can reserve about 1/2 cup of the blueberries and place them on top of the batter after you've filled your muffin tins. This will ensure you get the pretty look of the blueberries bursting on top of the muffins.

When it comes to blueberry muffins, I pledge Epsilon Alpha Tau (EAT). In fact, I'll be hazed ten times over for just a morsel of streusel topping. But the things I'd do for just a muffin top (and not one that grows on my own body), well, that's best suited for a different type of book. It's between me and the Muffin Man, and frankly, I don't kiss and tell. But I do share recipes, and this one for a standard, albeit orgasmic, blueberry muffin will replace Grandma's or anything you have been working from since you learned how to bake. The ratio of fruit vs. cakey goodness is award-winning, if I do say so myself. Like I'm actually tempted to take a trip to Party City and buy a ribbon every time I make these. Sorry, not sorry.

1 Preheat the oven to 350°F. Grease 16 muffin cups with nonstick spray.

2 In a large bowl, whisk together the all-purpose flour, whole-wheat flour, baking powder, baking soda, and salt to combine and set aside.

3 In the bowl of a stand mixer fitted with the paddle attachment, cream the butter and granulated sugar until light and fluffy, about 5 minutes. Add the eggs one at a time, beating well after each addition. Add the vanilla, lemon zest, lemon juice, and sour cream. Reduce the mixer speed to low and slowly add half the flour mixture, mixing until fully incorporated. Add the buttermilk and mix to combine. Add the remaining flour mixture and mix to combine. Remove the bowl from the stand mixer and fold in the blueberries with a rubber spatula.

4 Scoop the batter into the prepared muffin cups, dividing it evenly. Sprinkle with raw sugar. Bake for 30 to 35 minutes, rotating the pan halfway through, until the muffins are cooked through and golden. Transfer the pans to a wire rack for at least 5 minutes, then remove from the pan and transfer to the wire rack to cool completely.

Basic Bitch Banana Bread

PREP TIME: 25 MINUTES   **COOK TIME:** 1 HOUR 20 MINUTES
TOTAL TIME: 1 HOUR 45 MINUTES PLUS COOLING   **YIELD:** 1 LOAF (16 SLICES)

If there's one quick-and-easy baked good you can bring to a PTA or sorority fundraiser, it's banana bread. This is the loaf that was meant for popped collars, pearls, that picnic basket that looks like Dorothy's, and anyone named Karen. Or anyone named Dorothy, for that matter. Sounds basic enough. All you need are overly ripe bananas and a few other pantry staples to whip up a moist and dense delight that even banana haters typically enjoy. Walnuts are completely optional, though they're not something I ever turn down because nuts are supposed to be good for your cognitive function and I need all the help I can get. What's Dorothy's last name again? Topeka?

1   Preheat the oven to 350°F. Grease a 9 by 5-inch loaf pan with nonstick spray and line with parchment paper. Line a baking sheet with parchment paper.

2   Peel 4 bananas and place them on the prepared baking sheet. Roast for 20 minutes. Remove from the oven and transfer the bananas to a medium bowl; keep the oven on. Using a potato masher, mash until smooth. You should have about 1½ cups mashed banana. Set aside to cool.

3   In a large bowl, whisk together the flour, baking powder, baking soda, salt, and cinnamon to combine and set aside.

4   In the bowl of a stand mixer fitted with the paddle attachment, cream the butter and light brown sugar until light and fluffy. Add the eggs, one at a time, beating well after each addition. Add the mashed bananas and vanilla. Add half the flour mixture, followed by the buttermilk. Add the remaining flour mixture. Remove the bowl from the stand mixer and stir in the walnuts and chocolate, if using.

5   Pour the batter into the prepared loaf pan. Peel the remaining banana and slice in half lengthwise. Press the two halves into the top of the batter, cut-side up. Bake for 1 hour, until a toothpick inserted into the center of the loaf comes out clean. Remove from the oven and let cool completely. Slice and serve.

5 overripe large bananas

2 cups all-purpose flour

1 teaspoon baking powder

½ teaspoon baking soda

½ teaspoon kosher salt

1 teaspoon ground cinnamon

1 stick unsalted butter,
   at room temperature

¾ cup packed light brown
   sugar

2 eggs, at room temperature

1 teaspoon vanilla extract

2 tablespoons buttermilk

¾ cup chopped walnuts
   (optional)

½ cup chopped dark chocolate
   (optional)

JUST THE TIPS

Banana bread is the perfect treat to make if you need to use the bananas that you forgot about on your counter.

The riper the bananas get, the sweeter they become. Roasting the bananas brings out even more flavor.

Banana bread freezes very well. Slice into portions and freeze individually. When you're in a rush, you can grab a piece from the freezer and pop it in the microwave for 30 seconds for a quick breakfast or snack.

Acknowledgments

To Ms. Freda Hubbard Pittard, for teaching me how to learn.

To Mr. Paul Gibbons, for teaching me how to write.

To my parents, Joe and Robin, my sister, Sami, and my extended Skladany/Ell families, for teaching me how to laugh.

A special thanks to Anja Schmidt, Theresa DiMasi, Mary Gail Pezzimenti, Hana Asbrink, David Watsky, Patrick Sullivan, Matt Ryan, Jen Wheeler, Alexandra Utter, Carleigh Connelly, Caitlin O'Shaughnessy, Jill Slattery, Tatiana Lambert, and my entire Chowhound team. I couldn't have done this without you.

And to my BFFs Katie Russo, Joe Eletto, Art Rojas, Steven Nelson, Lani Chevlin, Sarah Inendino, Mallory Powell, Clare Kayden Hines, Julie Boor, Emily Robinson, Anisa Husain, Alyssa Cobb, Kellie Cullinan, Richard Del Pino, Andy Borgese, Travis O'Neill, Anthony Gianacakos, Lori Bassano Monserrat, Heather Bassano, Lorraine "Nana" Maurer, Lauren Coffaro, Cristina Contento Sutton, Allison Miller-Schwartz, Joanna Brahim, Nicole Blake Johnson, Filippa Harrington, Hilary Dowling, and Taylor Strecker, for putting up with all the Skladrama. ILYSM.

Index

Note: Italic page numbers indicate illustrations.

About the Author

Joey Skladany is a writer/editor, TV/radio personality, lifestyle expert, and former entertainment publicist who grew up in Naples, Florida. Currently, he is editor-at-large at CBS Interactive's Chowhound, where he contributes to the site's food and travel content. Prior to a career in writing, he was a publicist for TLC, serving as the PR lead for the network's highest-rated series, including *Here Comes Honey Boo Boo*, *My Strange Addiction*, and *My Crazy Obsession*. Joey attended Northwestern University, receiving a BA in communication studies with a minor in theater. In his spare time, he enjoys cooking (obviously), volleyball, traveling, worshipping Beyoncé, interior design, and perfecting his stand-up routine. When not in New York City, you'll typically find him on a beach.